COPING WITH A PICKY EATER

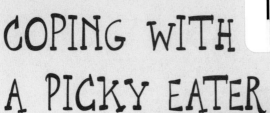

A GUIDE FOR THE PERPLEXED PARENT

D0069627

WILLIAM G. WILKOFF, M.D.

A FIRESIDE BOOK
Simon & Schuster

FIRESIDE
Rockefeller Center
1230 Avenue of the Americas
New York, NY 10020

Copyright © 1998 by William G. Wilkoff, M.D., F.A.A.P.

All rights reserved, including the right of reproduction in whole or in part in any form.

FIRESIDE *and colophon are registered trademarks of Simon & Schuster Inc.*

Designed by Jenny Dossin

Manufactured in the United States of America

10   9   8   7   6   5   4   3   2   1

Library of Congress Cataloging-in-Publication Data

Wilkoff, William G.

   Coping with a picky eater : a guide for the perplexed parent/
William G. Wilkoff.

   p.   cm.

   1. Children—Nutrition—Psychological aspects.   2. Food preferences.
I. Title.

RJ206.W786   1998

613.2'083—dc21   98-7846   CIP

ISBN 0-684-83772-2

In the interest of simplicity, we have used the pronoun "he" throughout to refer to the picky eater, although we recognize, of course, that being a picky eater is by no means a gender-specific phenomenon.

TO MY MOTHER,
who taught me to value common sense,
and
TO MY FATHER,
who encouraged me to write about it.

ACKNOWLEDGMENTS

I would like to thank the thousands of parents in Midcoast Maine who have allowed me to share in the care of their children. They have been candid in telling me when my suggestions haven't worked, and they have been eager to describe their serendipitous successes so that I can pass them on to other troubled parents. I am grateful for their patience when I blabbered on about my own children when it was their children who were sick. Their unfailing curiosity in wanting to know "How's the book coming, Doc?" kept me enthusiastic when I was discouraged about its progress.

Candace Watson, M.L.S., librarian at MidCoast Hospital in Brunswick, helped me find the references that I needed to support my experience-based conclusions. Deborah Brooks, M.S., R.D., here at the Bowdoin Medical Group, was kind enough to share her personal library with me, and to review the manuscript to make sure that the nutritional information and meal-planning suggestions made sense.

ACKNOWLEDGMENTS

Sydny Miner, my editor, deserves special thanks for her firm and experienced hand in guiding my stumbling steps as we turned a very rough draft into a finished manuscript. I hope that she forgives me for all those irritating E-mails asking when the book would finally hit the shelves.

Suzanne Gluck, my agent at International Creative Management, initially suggested that I write something about picky eaters while I was waiting for some of my other projects to appear in print. I thank her for the persistence that must have convinced the publisher that Maine had more to offer than lobsters and pine trees.

Finally, I would like to thank Marilyn, my best friend and wife of thirty years. Her devotion to our children and the management of our pediatric practice has allowed me to concentrate my energies on seeing sick children and their worried parents. I could not have written this book without the freedom that her hard work has provided me.

WILLIAM WILKOFF, M.D.
Brunswick, Maine

CONTENTS

HAVE YOU PICKED UP

THE RIGHT BOOK?

Do you often prepare two or three different menus for supper because your child continues to reject each of your offerings? Have you gotten tired of dumping full plates of food down the garbage disposal? Do you feed him canned spaghetti every evening because you know he will eat it?

Do mealtimes often end in arguments between you and your spouse over how much and what your child should be eating? Does your child often complain of bellyaches during meals? Have you resorted to bribery with stickers, treats, or toys just so your picky eater will eat some of his vegetables? Has your mother taken you aside and told you that she is worried because her grandson looks skinny and never cleans his plate?

If your child is between the ages of one and five years and doesn't eat as much as you think he should or seems to avoid the variety of foods that you think is healthy, you have in your hands a book that will help you understand and cope with this behavior. If meals have become times of tension and squabbling, I can show you how to create a dinner table atmosphere that will allow every family member to enjoy sitting down together again. Even if your child is only nine months old and you are beginning to wonder if he will ever broaden his range of favorite foods, you will find this book helpful, because you will find it also contains suggestions for prevention as well as management of picky eating.

SETTING THE STAGE

You may be parents who are both employed out of the home and are working with a day care provider who is feeding your child one or two meals per day. You may be a single parent and find yourself facing your child's picky eating alone, or you may share custody and must deal with eating behavior in situations over which you have little control. If you are adoptive parents, particularly if your child has come from a foreign country, you may be unsure how to respond to your child's food preferences and how to interpret his growth patterns. This book will help.

Picky eating is a behavior that almost every small child will exhibit some time before he turns six, and it is one of the most common topics of discussion at well-child visits in my pediatric office. Your child's failure to eat as heartily as you think he should is probably high on your list of parental worries.

In most cases picky eating will begin around age one. It begins to wane as the child gets into a school situation and starts to fall under the influence of peers and other role models he will find away from home, usually when he is three to five years old. For some children this is a lifelong pattern that will be evident even when they are in college. There are many children who will eat well most of the time and then, often inexplicably, will become very choosy for a few weeks or months. The advice in this book can be useful for all of these children from the occasional picky eater to the one whose eating habits are legendary in the family and around the neighborhood.

Coping with a Picky Eater is an appropriate resource for you even if you think that your child's eating behavior is normal, but your spouse, your mother, your in-laws, or your day care provider thinks that your child is a picky eater. You may find out that their perception is correct, or you may learn enough in these pages to be able to understand that your child's eating pattern is normal.

This book is *not* for the parents of a child with a chronic disease, severe emotional problems, or one whose diet must be significantly restricted by allergy or by physical limitations that make chewing or swallowing difficult. I have also excluded children from age nine to eighteen years because preadolescents and adolescents can have complex and often serious eating disorders that demand more than just effective parenting skills. These young people usually need a combination of medical management and psychotherapy, which is clearly beyond the scope of this book.

What you will learn as you read through these pages is that picky eating is a very common behavior among small children. You will learn how to determine if your child's eating habits fit into the range of this normal pattern, and you will learn if your style of parenting is contributing to the behavior. You will discover that there are several simple changes you can make in the way you present food to your child that help you avoid some of the nutritional pitfalls that picky eaters can fall into, and I will show you how you can create a family meal that is no longer an ordeal to be endured, but is instead an event that the entire family will eagerly anticipate and enjoy.

While this book is short enough to be read in a sitting or two, you will probably find that you will come back to it several times as your child grows and his eating patterns change and present new challenges. Since picky eating is a behavior that may persist for many months or even years, you will want to come back to some of the chapters again and again for booster shots of emotional strength as you work to bolster your coping skills. You will discover that *Coping with a Picky Eater* will become an important part of your parenting survival kit, a member of your support group that you can hold in your hand.

WHY *COPING* AND NOT *CURING?*

As soon as I decided to write a book for parents of picky eaters, I knew exactly what the title would be. For twenty-five years I had been working with families struggling with children who didn't eat the variety and quantity of food their parents thought they should. I learned quickly that these children were not going to give up their finicky ways because of anything that I was going to do. I didn't have any magic potion stashed away in my black bag that was going to make these stubborn little birds finish, or even start, eating their peas.

One doesn't cure something that is normal, and picky eating is normal behavior for children in the one- to five-year age group. However, in many families this "normal" behavior creates considerable havoc. Parents worry, concerned that their child is ill or that she is going to become ill because she isn't eating properly. Parents argue with each other about what to serve and how to punish or reward what they consider acceptable behavior. Meals are no longer fun for anyone in a family with a picky eater. Some children react by complaining of belly pain at the dinner table and a few even vomit because of the pressure to eat that they must endure.

Most parents feel responsible for their child's well-being and so feel obligated to get her to eat what they feel is a "balanced" diet in sufficient quantity every day. The problem occurs when there is a discrepancy between the parents' perceptions of what constitutes a healthy diet and the reality of what their child actually eats each day. Fearful that their child will become ill or stop growing, they panic and try a variety of desperate measures to get their picky eater to eat.

Often parents prepare three or four meals per sitting to get their picky eater to ingest something and to satisfy the wishes of other finicky family members. It is not uncommon for each person at the table to have a completely different selection of food on his plate, because the child may not be the only picky eater in the family. For example, Dad may be having steak, eight-year-old Martha is getting chicken because she and her friends have given up red meat, and Mom is just having a green salad because she is trying to lose weight. Four-year-old Robbie is being offered frozen pizza because everyone "knows" that he won't eat what the rest of the family is eating.

Other parents give their child a monotonous and unhealthy diet because that is what he will eat. In my practice macaroni and cheese and corn are particular favorites, and I know of many children who are served this "Nothing green, please" entrée five nights out of seven because they won't try anything else. I can recall one family that sheepishly admitted they had been offering their child a bowl of breakfast cereal every night for dinner for the three months before they came to see me. What begins as a "normal *childhood* behavior" often spirals into a chaotic and very abnormal *family* situation. The parent responsible for preparing the meal is asked to function well beyond the call of duty. Meals often degenerate into arguments as parents attempt to force the child into eating. Parents begin to yell at each other as they try to assign blame for their picky eater's frustrating behavior. The child may begin to complain that she doesn't feel well because that is the only way she knows how to stop the carnage.

Some parents are fortunate enough to be able to accept their child's picky ways without much concern and find something else to worry about, but they are in the minority. Most parents need some reassurance and coaching on how to cope with their child's finickiness. Sometimes I can be of help merely by examining the picky eater and reminding her parents how well she is looking and growing. However, I often find that I need to help parents set limits on their own and their child's behavior. I don't cure the child of her picky eating. I teach the parents coping skills. Maybe the child becomes a little less picky, but, more important, the atmosphere in the family improves and meals again become times to be enjoyed and not dreaded.

I was introduced recently to a woman who had been told that I was writing a book about picky eating. She said, "Our pediatrician just told me to offer our boys what I thought they should have and then not worry. They did just fine." Obviously, she didn't need to read my book. I would put her comment in the same category with Nancy Reagan's response to drugs: "Just say no!" It's the *correct* answer, but it is too simplistic for situations most of us face.

For a few parents it's easy to just say no: "No, I'm not going to fix three different menus for supper tonight." "No, I'm not going to worry because you didn't eat your green beans." "No, you can't have macaroni and cheese six times a week." But most of us need a little support and positive reinforcement when it comes to our child's behavior. We may be unsure *when* to say no and even *how* to say no. "No" is not a response that comes easily, but saying no effectively and appropriately is a skill that can be learned. You can learn that your child's natural appetite can be trusted. You can learn what a healthy diet actually consists of, how to offer what you want your child to eat, and you can learn when and how to say, "No, you are drinking too much juice" and "No, you can't have more macaroni and cheese until you have eaten those few peas that I put on your plate." No one is going to cure your picky eater for you, but you can learn how to deal with her behavior in a way that can return meals to their place among other enjoyable family experiences.

BEFORE YOU

READ ANOTHER WORD . . .

This book is written for the more than 90 percent of parents who have children who are physically, emotionally, and mentally healthy. If your child has a chronic illness or has already been identified as having a behavior problem, this book is not for you. In writing this book I begin with the assumption that your child is healthy. Before I can convince you that your child's eating habits are normal, we need to be sure that your child is well.

FIRST STOP: YOUR PEDIATRICIAN

If I were your pediatrician, I would have you come into the office, where I would examine your child and take some measurements, and maybe do some tests, like a simple blood count to rule out anemia, and a urinalysis to detect kidney problems and diabetes. However, I live up here on the coast of Maine and while I would enjoy the chance to meet you and examine your child, it just isn't practical. Therefore, before you read any further, I want you to be as sure as you can that your child is healthy. This may require a trip to the pediatrician in addition to your child's regular well-child (sometimes called health-maintenance) visits. Some simple blood and urine tests may be necessary to reassure both you and the pediatrician that things are just fine. Sometimes multiple visits may be necessary merely to obtain enough measurements to demonstrate that your child is growing adequately. It may cost you some money, but both you and the pediatrician must be convinced that your child is free of significant disease and growing normally before you can comfortably use the suggestions that make up the rest of this book.

MEASURING YOUR CHILD

When you go to the pediatrician, make it clear that you are concerned about your child's appetite and eating habits. Ask the doctor to weigh and measure your child and show you how he plots out on a standard growth chart. Hopefully, the pediatrician will have collected previous heights and weights so that you can see how your child is doing over time. If this is your first trip to this doctor, it is very important to bring along or, even better, have sent ahead of time your child's previous medical records, particularly any height and weight measurements. This effort on your part will make the visit much more valuable and possibly avoid the need for additional visits.

With the help of standard growth charts and some information about your families' body builds, your pediatrician should be able to reassure you that your child is neither too short nor too skinny. Of course, most of us would like our child to be at least "bigger than average." However, this is clearly impossible because only half of us can have a child that is bigger than average. Many factors influence how big a child is going to be, but the biggest factor seems to be heredity. If you and your spouse are big people and come from families that are big, then you are likely to have big children, but, of course, there are always exceptions—most of them normal. If one of you is big and the other is small, you roll the dice and anything can happen. Scientists know a little more about the heredity of size, but, take my word for it, the information is not solid enough to allow us to predict exactly how big your child should be.

If your child proves to be well below average in size when you go to the pediatrician, she may ask for the heights and weights of you and your spouse and estimates of the heights and builds of grandparents, aunts, and uncles on both sides of the family. This information may be quite helpful in determining that your child has a normal pattern. However, if your child has been adopted, you may or may not have any information about the size of his parents. You may have contact with the biological mother, but she may not have any information about the father's side of the family. If your child comes from another country, or is from an ethnic group that is not the same as yours, you and your pediatrician need to be aware of what their particular normal growth pattern is. As helpful as family body sizes and growth patterns can be, they are probably not worth opening sealed records or stirring up emotionally charged issues that have been put to rest.

It is a bit dangerous to look at just one set of measurements for reassurance, but if they are normal, you can probably read on with the assurance that my suggestions can be followed safely. However, other measurements at three- to six-month intervals might be helpful.

If your child's height is growing nicely parallel to one of the percentile lines and his weight is also moving along in a parallel path, even though it may be in a slightly lower percentile, I wouldn't worry. However, if the child's height and/or his weight is falling off his usual percentile line, then I might be concerned.

Remember that you should not put too much stock in a single set of measurements. A graph is made up of a collection of numbers. Any one number may have been measured inaccurately, or the child might have had an illness that temporarily affected his eating habits and/or rate of growth. If your child seems to be falling off his curves on the basis of one set of measurements, don't panic. Discuss the situation with the pediatrician and arrange to have some more measurements in the next few months. As long as the child seems healthy in all other respects, this is a sensible and prudent approach. Most of the time your patience will be rewarded with improved numbers at the next doctor's visit.

The doctor should perform a complete physical examination and ask you some questions about your child's body functions, particularly his urine and bowel habits. She should be aware of any significant past medical history, including frequent infections such as otitis (ears), bronchitis (lungs), and pharyngitis/tonsillitis (throat).

BLOOD AND URINE TESTS

I am usually not a great advocate of the routine use of laboratory tests in pediatrics, but one very common condition that can be associated with a decrease in appetite is iron deficiency anemia. Nature is particularly cruel when it comes to this disease because the cure for this anemia lies in eating a better diet, but the disease itself blunts the child's appetite and prevents him from solving the problem himself. Iron deficiency anemia usually can be detected by a simple office blood count and easily treated by giving a liquid iron supplement. If you're concerned about your child's lack of appetite, you should ask your pediatrician to order a hematocrit or hemoglobin test if she hasn't already suggested

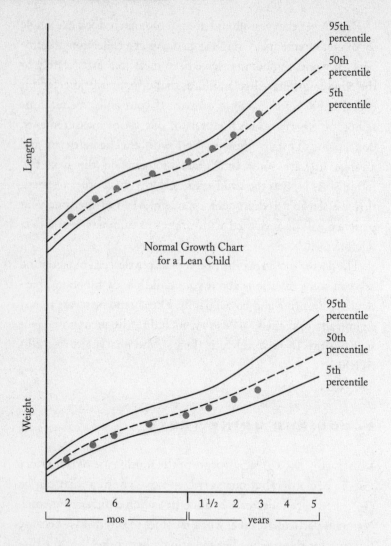

Normal Growth Chart
for a Lean Child

GRAPH A is the growth chart of a child who is well below average for both height and weight. In fact, he is actually underweight for his height and would look like a skinny little kid to everyone. However, he has always been this way and has continued to follow this pattern for a couple of years. He is a healthy but small child who is growing normally.

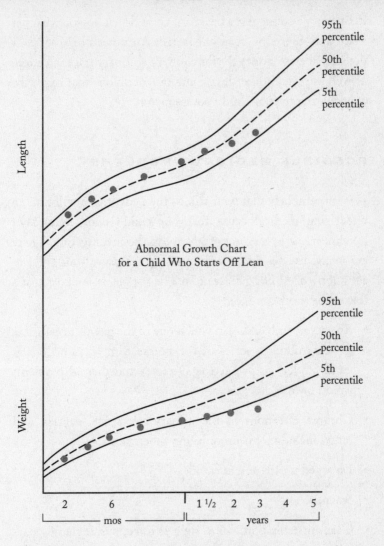

Abnormal Growth Chart
for a Child Who Starts Off Lean

GRAPH B is that of a young girl who began having urinary tract infections that had escaped diagnosis. You can see that for the first year she was growing normally, but her weight began to decline, and eventually she stopped growing in height. She had become a picky eater because she had developed a serious illness and her abnormal growth chart is the first clue.

it. She may also suggest a basic urine test depending on what her exam and questions have uncovered. An office urinalysis may detect diabetes, kidney dysfunction, or a urinary tract infection, as well as several other less-common conditions that might be contributing to your child's poor appetite.

POSSIBLE MEDICAL PROBLEMS

It is very unlikely that your trip to the pediatrician will find an underlying medical cause for your child's poor eating, but nonetheless it is very important to do the investigation. There are many diseases and conditions that can cause your child to eat poorly or to not gain weight. The list below includes just a few of the most common:

- Endocrine imbalance, in which one of the glands responsible for controlling a series of the body's complex functions is either under- or overactive. Diabetes and thyroid problems would fit into this group.

- Chronic infections of the urinary tract, ears, sinuses, and lungs, including pneumonia and tuberculosis.

- Enlarged tonsils and adenoids.

- Anemia.

- Gastrointestinal problems, such as infections, including parasites, inflammation (colitis), and constipation.

- Neurologic conditions such as cerebral palsy and mental retardation.

- Allergies and asthma.

- Heart disease.

Two of the conditions on this list deserve special mention. Forty to fifty years ago, tonsils, which are collections of lymph tissue on either side of the throat that help defend against infection, were removed at the least provocation. However, we now are much more conservative when it comes to recommending this surgical procedure. An excessive number of strep infections (more than four or five in a year) remains the one reason for tonsil removal that is agreed upon by most physicians.

Sometimes the tonsils are so large that they interfere with breathing (usually at night) and swallowing. You can imagine that a four-year-old with two tonsils the size of Ping-Pong balls might have trouble eating solid food. However, I am often surprised that many children with large tonsils eat just fine. The point is that removing enlarged tonsils merely because a child is a poor eater is very controversial. Most pediatricians, including myself, would not make this recommendation, although we realize that after the surgery the child *might* eat better. The tonsils do shrink as the child gets older, and are usually quite small by early adulthood. Unless your child has been diagnosed with sleep apnea (loud snoring interrupted by abnormally long pauses between breaths) or has chronic throat infections, it is not a good idea to remove tonsils for poor eating alone.

Constipation is often not included in a list of the causes of poor eating in children. Like iron deficiency anemia, it is a chicken-and-egg sort of problem. Children who eat abnormally small meals and lack variety in their diet are often constipated and children who are constipated are often picky eaters. The child who is constipated may have a poor appetite because he feels "full" all the time. When he does eat, his stomach enlarges and triggers a normal reflex called peristalsis. When these waves of muscular contractions travel down his intestines, they create a cramping sensation that can be very uncomfortable when they encounter stool that has been retained in his rectum.

Usually, the association between constipation and appetite is obvious, but sometimes neither parent nor pediatrician has thought to make the connection. If your child tends to be constipated, you should discuss this with the pediatrician. Severe cases may need to be treated with a combination of medication and behavior modification. While laxatives, enemas, and mineral oil may be helpful, these measures *should not be taken without specific directions from the pediatrician,* because improper use may be counterproductive and dangerous. However, if the constipation is mild, the recommendations in the rest of this book may solve the problem by improving the child's eating habits. Increasing fiber, decreasing milk consumption, and avoiding bananas and cheese seem to be the most helpful dietary changes when it comes to managing mild constipation.

POSSIBLE EMOTIONAL PROBLEMS

Even in very young children, emotional upset can cause loss of appetite. Depression is probably the most common of these problems, but it is at the top of a very long list of conditions in which mental health and appetite are intertwined. Sometimes the emotional disorder comes first, but there are occasions when excessive tension in the family surrounding the issue of nutrition can cause the child to eat poorly. Parents who continue to pressure their child to eat may be creating an atmosphere that discourages the child from eating. It's another Catch-22 situation: The child may not have had a nutritional problem in the beginning, but parental response has resulted in a situation in which the child really isn't eating adequately.

Often the tension in the family has nothing to do with the child's eating habits in the beginning, but it can ultimately affect his appetite. Imagine a home in which the parents are always quarreling and, in fact, do some of their worst fighting at dinnertime, or a home in which an alcoholic parent comes to the dinner table each evening drunk. It would not be surprising if a child who sits down to a meal with this kind of emotional turmoil swirling around him loses his appetite.

Before you read further in this book, take some time and think about your family's emotional climate. Have you or anyone else wondered about other aspects of your child's behavior? Is your marriage a happy one? Would you call your household stable? Is there alcoholism or other chemical dependency in the family? Has there been a recent death of a relative, friend, or even a pet? Has a friend of your child's moved away? Has there been a recent divorce or separation? If you are unsure, ask the pediatrician if she thinks your child's poor eating could be related to a broader emotional or family problem. This may help the doctor see the problem from a different angle and may give you both a good starting point for some very beneficial dialogue.

Over the years I have found that sometimes when a child is brought in because of poor eating the real problem is an unresolved emotional issue that involves some or all of the other family members. For example, do *you* and your spouse or partner have a healthy attitude toward food? Have you ever had an eating disorder? Do you still struggle with the problem? Could some of your concerns about your child's picky eating stem from concerns about your child inheriting or developing your problems? These are questions that should be discussed with your pediatrician (and a therapist or counselor if you still think that you have an eating disorder). Attempts at dealing with the issues of picky eating are fruitless until the underlying conflicts are resolved at least partially.

ADOLESCENTS AND THEIR WORLD

I must remind you that this book is for the parents of children ages one to five years and is *not* meant to be applied to the eating problems of adolescents. The problems that teenagers have with food and eating may have some of their roots in childhood, but the solutions to the problems are often complex and always difficult. On the one hand some parents complain that their teenage children (usually sons) are eating them out of house and home. On the other an increasing number of families are struggling with serious problems of body image in the form of eating disorders, which include anorexia nervosa and bulimia. These conditions are potentially life-threatening and are very difficult to manage. They are best handled with a team approach that includes physicians, psychiatrists, and nutritionists.

Attempts to apply this book's basic principles and strategies to older children with eating disorders are likely to fail and certainly could be dangerous. While eating disorders such as anorexia and bulimia are most common in adolescents, I have seen a troubling increase in the number of younger children in my practice who are overly concerned about being too heavy. If your child is a picky eater and you suspect it's because they think they are too heavy, do not follow the suggestions in this book without a full consultation with the pediatrician no matter how young the child is.

IT IS EXTREMELY IMPORTANT THAT YOU HEED THE ADVICE GIVEN IN THIS CHAPTER. IF YOUR CHILD IS EATING POORLY BECAUSE HE IS ILL, IT IS IMPERATIVE THAT HE GET APPROPRIATE MEDICAL ATTENTION PROMPTLY. IF YOU ARE GOING TO FOLLOW THE SUGGESTIONS THAT MAKE UP THE BULK OF THIS BOOK, YOU MUST BE CONFIDENT THAT YOUR CHILD IS HEALTHY. LINGERING DOUBTS ARE GOING TO MAKE IT DIFFICULT, IF NOT IMPOSSIBLE, TO CARRY THROUGH WITH THE STRATEGIES YOU ARE GOING TO LEARN IN THE SUBSEQUENT CHAPTERS. SO . . . GET YOUR CHILD CHECKED OUT AND READ ON!

A FEW OUNCES OF PREVENTION

If you are fortunate enough to have picked up this book while your child is still a babe in arms, if you are pregnant or planning to have another child, this chapter contains strategies to minimize picky eating as your child gets older. I am not going to promise that these strategies will completely prevent picky eating because it is often a behavior that some children seem to bring with them when they enter the world. However, since picky eating can also develop if parents create an environment that allows it to take hold and flourish, there is hope that you can head off some of these problem behaviors before they get too deeply rooted. By following the few simple suggestions in this chapter, you will be miles ahead of your less-enlightened friends when your child turns one.

SOLUTIONS BEFORE PROBLEMS BEGIN

1. *Separate sleeping and feeding.* Whether you are bottle-feeding or breast-feeding, do not use a feeding as a way to put your

child to sleep. Think about it: You are feeding your child so that he will grow, not so that he will sleep. This means that you should stop feedings before your child falls asleep. The child should be put to bed awake and then allowed to put himself to sleep. You may find it difficult in the beginning to achieve this goal, and I am afraid a discussion of the techniques involved is beyond the scope of this book. I suggest that you read Dr. Richard Ferber's *Solve Your Child's Sleep Problems* (Simon & Schuster, 1986) as a good first step in dealing with this issue. If you are successful in separating sleeping from eating, your child is less likely to drag breast-feeding or bottle-feeding into his second year, when it may interfere with his appetite for solids.

2. *Don't let your child hold his own bottle.* At about age four months, children who are bottle-fed begin to put their hands around the bottle. You should be pleased that your child is about to master another developmental milestone with this effort, but don't release your grip on the bottle. You may be tempted to allow your child to begin some of the responsibility for feeding himself. If he can hold his bottle, you won't have to hold him in your lap while he is eating; you can be free to catch up on some of the chores on your growing "to do" list. Eventually, this philosophy of nutritional independence is a good one, but there is a downside. If you allow your child to take complete control of the bottle, he will begin to think that it belongs to him, and when it comes time for weaning, he will be more upset because you will be trying to take something away that he has come to believe is his own. If you maintain control of the bottle, your child will realize that it is *your* bottle; you are merely using it to feed him. As he becomes more independent and ventures out into the world around him, the bottle will stay with you because you never let go.

This simple strategy can make weaning a more natural process and more easily accomplished. If you have been careful to keep a tight grip on the bottle, your child is much less likely to carry it with him into his second year and therefore is less likely to become a picky eater with a serious drinking problem.

3. *Almost never put juice in a bottle.* If your infant has been troubled by constipation, your pediatrician may suggest giving him juice to alleviate the problem. If the baby is too young (less than six months) to take a cup successfully, you will have to give him the juice in a bottle. However, if you are giving him juice as just another new addition to his diet, then wait until he can take it from a cup. This strategy avoids one more kind of bottle to remove as he gets older and helps prevent him from over-drinking juice and consequently blunting his appetite.

4. *Introduce a cup at about five months of age.* Most children are eager to try drinking dilute juice (apple or white grape) from a cup as early as five months of age. You will probably notice that if you are holding a child in your lap and drinking from a glass at the same time, he will want to share it with you. Let him try! Obviously, be selective in what you offer, but use an open cup or glass because it will be easier for him to learn to drink from that than from one with a spout or lid. Save these spill minimizers for when he is able to hold the cup himself. Until then put up with the mess. A sponge and a towel is all that you need.

This early start with a cup will give your child plenty of time to perfect the skill before he reaches his first birthday and will make it less likely that he will be an overdrinker and a picky eater.

5. *Don't quit!* If your baby is like most other babies, he will not be very adventurous when it comes to new foods. Some experts call this aversion "neophobia," or fear of the new. What this means to you is that you must expect that your child will reject most foods you offer the first time, and the second time, and the third. *Don't quit!* Unless your child has an obvious allergic reaction (such as hives, skin rash, vomiting, or diarrhea) when you give him a food, you should continue to offer him the rejected

food, week after week. Eventually, your baby will accept it, although it may never be a favorite.

Scientists confirm that children will respond to repeated exposure by eventually trying foods that they once rejected. If you quit after one or two failed attempts at a new food, you are contributing to your child's picky eating as he gets older. Don't force-feed him, just be persistent as you introduce new foods. Begin with very small amounts. If your child doesn't eat any of his pureed peas when you offer them to him, don't leap up and offer him a jar of his favorite yellow squash. He won't starve or become malnourished waiting until the next meal, even if it is twelve hours away. It may take fifteen or twenty exposures before he will begin to sample some of the foods he initially spit out, but in the long run your persistence will be rewarded.

6. *Please let him do it himself.* As your baby gets to be eight or nine months of age, he may start rejecting foods that he would once eat with relish. You also may find that he is unwilling to accept any foods that are lumpy in texture, which can make moving through the different "stages" of commercial baby food very difficult.

The solution to both of these problems is to take advantage of your child's developing dexterity and natural desire to put things in his mouth. Begin to offer him foods that he can pick up with his fingers and feed to himself. You don't need to wait until he has any certain number of teeth (if any), but you do need to be careful that he has sufficient oral coordination to meet the challenge. Some babies who have no teeth at all can chew many solid foods with which others who have four or five teeth may have difficulty.

Most children will enjoy being in control and will eagerly feed themselves pieces of food that they would reject if given to them smooshed up in a lumpy puree. Of course, you must think of safety and only offer foods that will easily soften and dissolve in his mouth. Overcooked pasta and vegetables make good first choices. When a child has mastered a pincer grasp, Cheerio-type cereals can be fun. Before that developmental stage has been reached, a heel of French bread or a bagel offers the child something he can grip and gum. Obviously, the child should never be eating unattended in case he begins to choke on even the most carefully prepared solids.

You should also begin to trust your baby with his own utensils. Thickening foods to a consistency that will stick to an inverted spoon will allow your child the chance to perfect these self-feeding skills. Of course, if he begins to use his fork and spoons as weapons or toys, remove them and try again the next day. I don't think that it is a good idea to allow your child to play with his utensils away from the table, as some experts suggest. If you maintain a no-nonsense, matter-of-fact, somewhat businesslike attitude toward those feeding aids, so will your child.

Of course, this combination of finger-feeding and early attempts at utensil use are going to create a horrible mess, but let it happen. Wear a raincoat; put an old shower curtain down on the floor under his high chair; stock up on paper towels and sponges. You have a baby now, and I hope someone warned you that your house would look a little different than when you were childless. By allowing your child to control some of his feeding, you will be taking an important step toward that hardest of all parenting challenges, "letting go." You will find that you and your baby will enjoy mealtimes more and you will be well on your way toward coping with the more serious picky eating that awaits you in the second year.

NOT SO GREAT EXPECTATIONS

One of the biggest problems that we have as parents is that we are prone to unrealistic expectations when it comes to our children. Some of this delusion comes from our natural inclination to want what we think is best for our children. We want them to be blessed with all of our good attributes and inherit none of our deficiencies. However, many of our expectations are flawed by our unfamiliarity with the range of behavior of normal children. Many of us were raised as only children or were too self-absorbed to remember much about our siblings. If you are a first-time parent, you may not have been around small children since you were a child yourself and now you are expected to be an expert. You may know enough to realize that you shouldn't expect a three-year-old to quote Shakespeare (although, of course, yours does), but you may not be aware that most of them don't need to eat three square meals per day. This chapter is an attempt to match up some of your expectations about small children with reality so that coping with your picky eater will be less of a strain. If I can convince you that many of your child's behaviors that concern you are really normal, we will have taken a big step toward easing your job as a parent.

WHAT IS NORMAL BEHAVIOR?

1. AFTER THEIR FIRST YEAR CHILDREN'S GROWTH SLOWS DOWN CONSIDERABLY.

The growth of an infant in the first year is explosive. A typical newborn starts out weighing seven pounds and measuring nineteen inches in length. At one year he will have nearly tripled his weight to twenty pounds and grown almost a foot to be thirty inches long. By the time a child reaches her second birthday, she is growing only about one-tenth as rapidly as she did her first year. As a new parent you may come to expect this phenomenal growth rate to continue into the preschool period. It will not happen. If it did, your child would have a serious medical problem.

2. AFTER THE FIRST YEAR YOUR CHILD NEEDS RELATIVELY FEWER CALORIES.

As your child gets older, her body becomes leaner; in simple terms she loses her "baby fat." Her new body proportions require relatively less energy to function. For the preschool child this means that she needs only half as many calories per pound of body weight than she did as a baby. This why the two- to five-year-old may appear to be eating less as she gets older.

3. CHILDREN "STREAK EAT."

Young children will develop an affection for certain foods that may remain favorites for weeks or months or years and then inexplicably fall out of favor without warning. Children may eat very well for a few days and then just pick for a week. It is the unusual child who will eat a wide variety of foods in consistent quantities day in and day out.

4. BABIES ARE BORN WITH A NATURAL PREFERENCE FOR SWEET AND A DISLIKE FOR SOUR.

All of the other preferences or tastes for things are learned. Breast milk is intended to be your child's first food and it is *very* sweet. By repeated exposure you can modify your child's preferences for most foods. However, she may always prefer sweet things when given a choice.

5. CHILDREN ARE WARY OF NEW FOODS.

Although toddlers are prone to pick up and put strange things into their mouths that they shouldn't, such as Grandma's heart pills or those red berries in the neighbor's yard, they are very resistant to trying new foods. It just isn't in their nature. This does not mean that you shouldn't offer them new things to try, but your expectations that they will try them should be low. For the child who is a hard-core picky eater, I wouldn't suggest offering something new more than once or twice a week; you're not trying to look for trouble, just trying to make a point. Once you get mealtimes to be more pleasant for all concerned, you can become more adventuresome. Until then help your child by allowing her to have more success at eating by avoiding too many strange things in too short a period of time.

6. YOUNG CHILDREN USUALLY EAT ONLY ONE AND ONE-HALF TO TWO MEALS PER DAY.

If you are expecting your toddler or preschooler to pack down *three square meals* each day, you are going to be sorely disappointed. This means that your child may eat a good breakfast, a so-so lunch, and then next to nothing for dinner and be perfectly healthy.

7. YOUNG CHILDREN'S APPETITES SEEM TO DECLINE AS THE DAY GOES ON.

This is very important for the working parent to understand. Exactly why children eat less well late in the day is unclear. It may simply be that they have already consumed the necessary calories and their appetite shuts down, or it may be that they are more tired than hungry.

We all enjoy watching our children eat, and this characteristic daily decline in a young child's eating pattern can be very frustrating for the parent who is out of the home most of the day. On days that you work, it is possible that you may never see your child eat if you leave before his breakfast and get home after his appetite has passed, which could be as early as 4:30 or 5:00 P.M. If your child is in day care, it is likely that the day care provider will be the only one who gets to see your child really eat, particularly if your child gets his breakfast at day care.

If you or your spouse finds it very upsetting that you don't get to see your child eat at all, I have two suggestions. First, change your work schedules to make breakfast a family meal. I realize this may not be feasible if you must commute a long distance or be at work when the rest of the world is just getting out of bed. More often, it may simply mean getting out of bed twenty minutes earlier. The other solution would be to have the home parent or the day care provider videotape your child eating breakfast and/or lunch for showing later in the day. In addition to providing hard evidence, it may provide an enjoyable form of evening entertainment when you've already seen the *Seinfeld* rerun twice before. Of course, the child should not be told why the video is being made. The event should be low-key, and no mention made of what and how he is eating.

8. NOT EVERYONE LOVES TO EAT.

You may already know this but may have trouble applying it to your own child. Just as there is a wide variety of body shapes and sizes, there is a wide spectrum of appetites strung out across the population of children (and adults). Some people love to eat and move it near the top of their priority list for the day. Others only eat to stay alive and seem to get little pleasure out of the process. Fortunately, most of us enjoy eating but keep it in perspective when it comes to the rest of our lives. Certainly, there are children who were picky for the first six years of their life and then as if by magic suddenly become voracious eaters. This kind of change is most noteworthy in the adolescent male, but it can happen at any time to girls as well. However, there are children who will remain indifferent to eating for their entire lives. Unless you enjoy failure it is unwise to try to change these people.

9. YOUR CHILD'S FUTURE SUCCESS AS AN ATHLETE DOES NOT HINGE ON HIS SKILLS WITH A FORK AND SPOON.

We all want our children to enjoy success in their lives. For many of us that takes the form of dreaming that our child will be a college or professional athlete. This is one of the more unreasonable expectations that parents harbor. It is so prevalent that there is little hope of extinguishing it. However, please don't make the connection between eating performance and athletic ability. Your child has just as good a chance of making it in the major leagues whether or not he eats broccoli during the next twelve months.

Use this chapter as a "reality check." If parenting a picky eater continues to be a challenge, come back to this little chapter and read it again . . . and again.

NOT TO WORRY

This is probably the most important chapter in the book. If by the time you have finished reading it you are convinced that your child's eating habits—annoying as they may be—are perfectly normal and that it is not your job to get your child to eat, then using the rest of the book will not be difficult for you.

Accepting a new role will not be easy. Certainly it's going to be an upstream swim. During the first few months of life, it *was* your job as a parent to make sure that your child was taking in enough calories to thrive. It can be a scary time for a parent. Sometimes you just can't trust a baby in the first year to take in the calories that they should. If you were breast-feeding, it may have even been an experience you remember as harrowing. It may have taken your baby three days to figure out how to latch on to your nipple. Engorgement may have been painful and your breast became so hard that he couldn't nurse. Without little ounce markings on your breasts to let you know how much your child was taking, you probably worried that you didn't have enough milk. You may have heard horror stories about breast-fed babies who weren't getting enough milk and almost died of starvation or dehydration right in the middle of suburbia. Your pediatrician may have told you that you should supplement with formula because your baby wasn't gaining weight fast enough, or you may have had to stop nursing completely for a variety of good and bad reasons. While you understood that breast milk was the best thing to feed your baby, the feeling that only you—the nursing mother—could feed your baby may have become an unbearable burden.

If your baby was bottle-fed, you may have struggled to find a nipple that he would take readily and that would flow at just the right speed. He may have been intolerant of one or more formulas, and it may have seemed as if you would never find one that he could take without spitting up or getting crampy.

There are unusual medical conditions that crop up in the first few months of life that can interfere with a baby's ability to feed and gain weight adequately. Fortunately, these conditions are rare, but it is during the first year of life, and usually in the first six months, that they become apparent. For this very reason this book is not written for your child's first year. Do not try to apply its principles to feeding an infant.

By the time your child has reached his first birthday, the likelihood of him having some undiscovered birth defect is extremely rare. If he has managed to gain weight and grown in length, and is developing normally according to your pediatrician, you *should* be ready for that leap of faith into your new role as a parent who is content to be a presenter of food, but you aren't. You are afraid to leave your old job of getting food into your child. You worry . . .

WHAT ARE YOU SO WORRIED ABOUT?

1. HE WILL STARVE.

Is this really a rational concern? Step back and look at your child. You say you can see his ribs? That's normal. Starvation is a process that takes months to occur. The children of the Third World who are photographed by the media have probably been without adequate nutrition since birth. They have had little if any medical care and have become ill in their debilitated state. Below is a list of the top six causes of death in early childhood (ages one to four) in this country. Do you see starvation on that list? No. With the hundreds of thousands of picky eaters in this country, you would think that if starvation were a real danger to our children's health, it would have made the list. It didn't.

1. Accidents
2. Birth defects
3. Cancer
4. Homicide
5. Heart disease
6. Pneumonia and influenza

Starvation is not something that will kill your child because he hasn't eaten a green vegetable in six weeks. Your child has gotten good medical attention. The biggest difference between your child and the starving Somalian is that your child has been offered food and drink on multiple occasions, every day.

Yes, there are children who starve to death in North America, but they are almost always products of parents or families where there is significant mental illness or families that have shunned traditional medical care. Sometimes parents become obsessed with unusual dietary practices or religious solutions to significant medical problems and eventually starve their child by withholding an adequate diet or creating dietary rules that aren't compatible with a child's biologic requirements. The practices of these religious fanatics and food faddists are a real risk to the health of small children. Sadly, a child trapped in a family like this may die before there are any obvious signs of malnutrition in the adults.

I am going to make an assumption that by sitting down to read this book, you have demonstrated yourself to be a rational person and not likely to engage in bizarre forms of punishment that involve withholding food and water from your child. Furthermore, if you have taken your child to a pediatrician and continue with follow-up visits, you have bought yourself a pretty darn good insurance policy against starvation.

2. HE WON'T EAT THE RIGHT THINGS UNLESS I FEED HIM.

Nothing could be farther from the truth; children come into the world with some quality-control features already built in. Scientists have provided us with ample evidence that takes you off the hook when it comes to feeding your child. There are two very important scientific studies that should help build your trust in your child's natural appetite. The first of these was done way back in 1938 by a pediatrician named Clara Davis. It involved fifteen children who were presented a variety of food from which they were allowed to select their own diet. The experiment lasted for six months for most of the children and longer for some. Records were kept about what the children ate and how they grew. At the end of the experiment, it was clear that children did an excellent job of balancing out their diet when they were presented with a variety of healthy alternatives that did not include junk food.

They may have eaten large amounts of one foodstuff in the beginning and gone on eating jags of one sort or another, but over the long haul their diet was a healthy one and they grew well.

I am sure it must have been hard for some of the adults to sit by and watch as these children did their magical balancing act. Just as it may be difficult for you to watch your child steadfastly refuse to eat what seems to you to be a balanced diet. As this experiment shows, the problem is that we as parents are sitting too close to the problem. We are looking at the trees and missing the forest. We need to step way back and look at the whole picture that evolves over a period of many months, or maybe even years. Trust me, this is impossible for us to do. We are too emotionally involved. You must rely on the observations of scientists like Clara Davis and the practical experience of physicians like myself who have watched a generation or two of alleged poor eaters grow into healthy adulthood.

If you aren't convinced by Clara Davis's experiment, if you thought it was too long ago, if you wondered what would happen with today's children, who have the great temptation of junk food not available back in 1938, then there is a more recent study done by Dr. Lean L. Birch and her associates, published in the prestigious *New England Journal of Medicine* in 1991. In this experiment involving preschool children who attended a day care facility, the menu that was offered included things like cookies, graham crackers, brownies, and corn chips. Again, the children showed great variability and unpredictability in their choice of foods, and at any given meal their daily energy intake, as measured in calories, was relatively constant. In other words even if you offer children a diet with a few little treats in it they will still eat properly in the long run. The message is very clear. These scientists close their article with this sentence: "As revealed by Clara Davis 60 years ago, the successful feeding of children is best accomplished by providing them with a variety of healthful foods and allowing them to eat what they wish." (author's emphasis)

As you might imagine, there are always scientists who will quibble with the experiments of others; this skepticism is a healthy part of science. Drs. Davis and Birch may receive some criticism for their handling of statistics, but the vast majority of pediatricians and nutritionists have found that their own every-day observations of normal children are supported by these two experiments. Young children *can* be trusted to eat properly if they are offered ample food that includes a balanced variety of nutritional elements.

3. HE WON'T GROW UP TO BE BIG AND STRONG.

Unless you are withholding food from your child, his ultimate height and body build are more function of the genes that you have donated to him than what you have fed him. The next time you are at a wedding or a graduation, just observe the families that are around you. The tall parents have tall children and the short parents have short children. Sure, there are exceptions, but in general your child's final height is going to be a result of the unique collection of DNA that you and your spouse have combined in the process of conception. Of course, if a child is suffering from starvation, eventually his growth will be stunted. However, remember that your child isn't starving.

Body build is also inherited. Although there are always exceptions, thin parents are going to have lean children and chunky parents are going to produce children on the pudgy side of things. My father and I are lean people, and so I was not surprised when my son also didn't seem to gain much weight. It was a bit scary for his mother and me to watch him suit up for hockey games against young men who outweighed him by fifty pounds, but our patience was rewarded. There wasn't anything my son or I could do about his size until he was nearing the end of puberty and his body was ready to respond to the natural forces of hormones and genetic predetermination that were going to give him an adult and muscular body. At age twenty his body was ready to respond to weight lifting. As a teenager his body just wasn't capable of building substantial amounts of muscle. It wasn't in his genetic makeup. He had classmates whose bodies had matured earlier, not because their parents fed them better food, but because their parents had passed them different genes. Remember you can't make a silk purse out of a sow's ear and you're not going to make a sow's ear out of a silk purse.

So please don't worry about your child growing up to be big and strong. He will be as big as his special genetic makeup is going to allow, and he will be as strong as he wishes to make himself once he has reached puberty. Your efforts at force-feeding will not only fail, but they are bound to be counterproductive.

4. HE WILL GET SICK.

Yes, children who are malnourished are more vulnerable to serious infection. Measles is a disease in which the risk of death is significantly greater for the child who is malnourished. Death as a result of diarrheal illness, though it is common in third world countries where clean water and adequate sanitation are in short supply, is rare in North America and Europe. There is no evidence I know of showing that picky eaters who are managed properly are more susceptible to disease. You have been to the pediatrician who is following your child closely. She has reassured you that your child is not suffering from malnutrition and that he is at no greater risk of illness than his playmates. Even if your child has a number of food allergies, the management of his eating behavior can be straightforward; the only difference is that you will be selecting the diet that you offer your child from a shorter list. The basic principle of allowing the child to accept or refuse the offering remains the same.

There are some medical conditions that seem to be more common in picky eaters. I have noticed that children often have bowel problems when they are allowed to pursue their picky eating by parents who only offer them what they want to eat. This usually appears as constipation, which is associated with an excess of milk and cheese and not enough whole grains, fresh fruit, and vegetables. Children who drink juice to excess often have loose stools. However, if your child is presented a balanced diet and a rational set of limits, he will be no more vulnerable to disease than the child next door who seems to be a robust eater.

There are also some conditions that parents may be concerned are caused by their child's eating pattern. For example, many children experience periods of noticeable hair loss. There are several likely causes for this condition, known as alopecia, including severe protein malnutrition. The most common causes are "We don't know why" and nervous hair-pulling or hair-twirling by the child. Picky eating, however, is not a cause, although, the first question that parents ask is, "Is my child losing his hair because of his poor diet?" The answer is yes, in severe forms of malnutrition the hair can change color and fall out, but, no, that's not why your child is losing his hair. Skin rashes are another symptom that concern parents of picky eaters. Yes, in some forms of vitamin deficiency that go along with malnutrition skin rashes can occur, but, no, your picky eater's rash is not telling us that he is missing some important vitamin or mineral. More likely it is a viral infection, an allergic reaction, or an inherited sensitivity such as eczema.

5. HE'S NOT EATING BECAUSE HE'S SICK.

Is your child's chronic poor appetite a symptom of some terrible disease that he has had since birth or is developing? Now, here is something *real* to worry about. Loss of appetite is often a sign of illness, whether it is infection, metabolic imbalance, or some internal malformation. However, most children who are picky eaters have nothing wrong with them in the medical sense. If your child has been seeing a pediatrician on a regular basis for well-child care, and has no other symptoms such as unexplained fevers, chronic diarrhea, or cough, you probably have no cause for concern. But if your child's picky eating habits are a change from her regular patterns, especially if accompanied by other physical symptoms or changes in behavior, a trip to the doctor for a thorough examination, and possibly some additional tests, is a good idea. At the end of that process, you should be convinced that your child is not a picky eater because there is something wrong with him.

However, you may have some lingering concerns that there is still something wrong with your child. These doubts are normal, but when they are so strong that they prevent you from setting limits on your child's behavior and getting on with the coping strategies that I will suggest, then you need to seek other medical opinions to confirm that your child is healthy and perhaps consider psychological counseling for yourself and possibly your child. Some of us just worry too much for our (and our children's) own good. Admitting that irrational worrying is your problem is an important first step, and should be followed by seeking assistance from trained mental health practitioners.

6. HE WON'T EVER DEVELOP A TASTE FOR THINGS.

Are you worried that because your child doesn't eat a variety of foods now, when he grows up he will continue to be a picky eater? This may be a legitimate concern. Children come into the world with a preference for sweet-tasting, fatty, and creamy foods and an aversion to sour-tasting ones. They begin to enjoy stronger, more-complex tastes as they get older, but initially they have a rather sensitive palate that can be overwhelmed by the spicy, bitter, and acidic foods adults have learned not only to tolerate but to enjoy. Some scientists have postulated that this aversion of the nonsweet may have evolved as a mechanism to protect small children from toxic substances in their environment. Unfortunately, any pediatrician will tell you that even the pickiest eater can still manage to find and eat enough poisonous material to get into trouble before its bad taste prompts him to stop.

Children are by nature wary of new things, including food. This "neophobia" usually diminishes with age, but some adults continue to be unadventurous eaters. Think of your own experiences and how often you hear people say something like "You know, I didn't develop a taste for raw tomatoes until that summer after my sophomore year in college" or "My wife embarrassed me into eating broccoli for the first time, and now I love it." Adolescence is a time of change and often heralds the expansion of a young person's diet. Usually, it is just the amount of food consumed that increases, but sometimes they are also more willing to try new things, particularly as their circle of friends and experiences expands.

As you will learn, forcing your child to eat things is not going to make him like a variety of foods. In fact, he may just rebel and refuse to eat something later on just because he was made to eat them at one point in his life. I think the strategies that I will offer in this book give your child the best chance of developing a broad taste for things as he gets older.

If you make too much of a fuss about what your child doesn't eat, he may take on the role of picky eater as something to be proud of. He will become famous in the family and around the neighborhood as the child who doesn't eat anything. He will become renowned for his feats in avoiding vegetables. He will become so good at it that it will become a badge of honor, a set of skills that makes him more important than other children.

I can remember one mother telling me that they always kept

a can of corn for her son in the glove compartment of her car so that it wouldn't be forgotten when they traveled to family gatherings for the holidays. It got to be a standing joke that they never arrived for dinner empty-handed. They always had Mitchell's can of corn because he wouldn't touch anything green. This can became an image that will last for a lifetime, a self-fulfilling prophecy. Even if he wants to change later on, there is some embarrassment in admitting how foolish he was for all those years. So, yes, there is a risk of becoming a lifelong picky eater. Mismanagement of the problem in childhood may be a key factor in the persistence of this unpleasant behavior. Following the basic suggestions in this book are your best hope for your child avoiding a lifelong career of picky eating.

7. "CHILDREN ARE STARVING IN ———."

You may have been raised to appreciate the food that you were given because your parents or grandparents could remember a time when they didn't have enough food. They may have been products of the Depression or come from an economically deprived background and would never be able to think of food as something that should be wasted or thrown away. Although their standard of living possibly had risen to a point where there was little need to worry, there were still millions of people scattered throughout the world for whom food was in short supply. When I was growing up, my parents used to refer to the "starving Armenians." Now we might cite the Somalians or the Biafrans, but there will always be millions of people who finish every day without enough food.

You worry that your picky eater has not developed the respect for food that has been passed down through your family. While this sort of concern is not on a par with other, more serious life-and-death issues, it does have some merit. I think that we all need to share with our children a concern for those less fortunate than ourselves. The question remains of exactly how to achieve this goal with a picky child, especially when it is clear that there is no lack of food in the household or in the child's own experience of the outside world. Initial efforts should make the distinction between being choosy about food and being wasteful. Using leftovers instead of throwing them away makes an important statement that food is not a limitless resource to be squandered. Your child will see that you can't always predict how much the family will eat, and sometimes there is a solution if you have prepared too much. Eventually, someone will introduce your child to the concept of ecological awareness and conservation. Wouldn't it be best if his first lessons were learned at home? Consider the message that you are sending to your child when he watches you prepare and then discard three or four different menus until you stumble on the one he will eat. The way that you behave around food and what you say about food also set an example. If you say a blessing before meals, you probably already include a reference to food as a gift to be treasured. In chapter 10, I will show you how to set limits on your child's behavior (and your own) that will not only promote healthy eating habits and a respect for the value of food, but also keep wastage to a minimum. But do not try to talk your child into finishing his peas to help the starving Somalians. It won't work.

We all worry, some of us more than others. There is always something that you can worry about. I hope that I am beginning to convince you that your picky eater is not one of those things that you need to worry about. Don't be concerned if you still have some things that concern you. There is more evidence to help you set your mind at ease.

GETTING READY

TO TAKE THE LEAP

I'm sure we haven't left all of your worries behind. Around every corner lurk those second thoughts that can discourage you from becoming a confident parent who can leave the responsibility of eating to her child. The transition from taking responsibility for what your child eats to allowing him to make his own choices is not an easy one. It can be very uncomfortable and maybe even threatening to watch your child not-eat,* particularly if he is on the thin side. I speak from some experience. My wife and I have a son who is an excellent hockey player. He began skating the same year he walked. He quickly picked up the skills he needed to excel on the ice, but he was skinny. By the time he got into high school, he was as tall as his peers but he weighed barely one hundred pounds and was being asked to knock heads and bodycheck guys outweighing him by sixty to

*To make this book easier to write, and I hope read, I have coined a few words. The first of these is "not-eat." This simply is the act of not ingesting food. In its most aggravating form, it is done at the dinner table, but it can be done all over the house.

eighty pounds. He was not a great eater and for years it was difficult for us as parents to sit by quietly at mealtimes while he ate less than we hoped he would. I wish I could tell you that I never said anything. On a very few occasions, I spoke up and always regretted it later. If I said, "Nick, are you sure you don't want to have another hamburger?" he knew that the unspoken ending of the sentence was "because you need to be bigger if you want to keep up with hockey." It didn't make him eat any better, and sometimes my implication created an unpleasant scene at the dinner table. We knew he was healthy; we just wanted him to be heavier so that he wouldn't be severely injured playing a sport he dearly loved. In the long run we held our tongue (most of the time). His appetite came along when he got to college and at over six feet tall and 175 pounds, he is bigger and stronger than I am.

ASSEMBLING YOUR
SUPPORT GROUP

Relinquishing control is very difficult. To some extent it is unnatural, a total about-face from what you have just been through as the parent of an infant. You may need a shoulder to lean on, one you may not get from your parents or even your own spouse. Here are some suggestions on whom you might include (or exclude) in your support group as you enter this difficult phase of coping with a picky eater.

GRANDPARENTS

Everyone likes to see children eat and enjoy their food. Grandparents in particular get great pleasure in watching their grandchildren eat. While I may be able to convince *you* that it is okay to sit by and watch your child not-eat, I am going to have a lot more trouble with your parents or your in-laws. You may have already heard the mutterings of a grandmother that her grandchild is going to get sick if he doesn't start eating better. A grandfather may have voiced his concerns that his grandson won't carry on the great family football tradition if his appetite doesn't improve.

Grandparents mean well, but they don't have very good memories when it comes to raising children. They sometimes forget how difficult child-rearing can be. Grandparents may pull an about-face in attitude toward eating with their grand-children. The rules that they enforced so tenaciously when they were raising you may strangely not apply to their grandkids. Sometimes grandparents view the practice of allowing their grandchildren to eat whatever they wish as an inalienable right of grandparenthood. This may be of little consequence if your child sees his grandparents only once or twice a year. However, if Grandma is also a frequent baby-sitter or day care provider, she may sabotage your efforts to establish sensible limits by offering "forbidden" snacks and refusing to supply a variety of healthy foods.

One of our more positive images of a grandmother is that of a slightly plump, gray-haired woman with a cheerful smile and a passion for baking cookies for her grandchildren. To expect a grandmother not to exercise her prerogative to allow her grand-children to ignore the green beans and eat as much of her deli-cious baked goods as possible is unrealistic.

If grandparents have the attitude that your child will out-grow his picky eating and for now you should let him have whatever he wants to eat or drink whenever he wants it, they are only half right. Yes, your child is likely to outgrow his picky behavior, but avoiding the challenge of limit-setting is not going to help you either modify or cope with the problem. Sometimes this grandparental sabotage is done unconsciously and, unfortunately, sometimes it is not, but don't count on your parents or in-laws to be members of your support group as you get closer to the leap. But hang on and have strength. Loan them your copy of this book or, even better, buy one for them. Dog-ear this chapter and have them read it. It may help.

YOUR SPOUSE

Your role as a parent is merely to present the food and leave the rest up to the child, but you are probably part of a parenting team. Your partner in parenting may not have bought into the concept. This difference can present serious problems and must be resolved.

First, it is not fair to the child to present two different approaches to his eating behavior. Children look to their parents for guidance, and when they sense dissension it can be very unsettling for them. In these early years your child must have confidence in his parents if he is going to have confidence in himself. If you must argue about any issue (including eating patterns), please don't do it within earshot of your child, and certainly don't do it at the dinner table.

While I have no data to support my observation, over the years I've found that there is no gender bias when it comes to having difficulty accepting this approach to feeding children. In other words I see just as many families in which the father is the one having trouble watching his child not-eat as I do families in which the mother is the parent with the problem.

Fathers appear to be more outspoken about the problem, while mothers tend to be more indirect in their approach. Fathers seem more likely to take the "You will eat what we put in front of you or else" attitude. Mothers, on the other hand, often keep fixing meal after meal in hopes of finding something that the child will eat. Either approach is equally bad. On the one hand the confrontational approach can backfire and the child may start vomiting or develop other behavioral problems.

On the other hand the "Whatever you want, dear" attitude is unfair to the rest of the family and runs the risk of creating an unhealthy nutritional situation. I have also observed that the child probably won't eat what he asked for, anyway.

The bottom line is that both parents need to present a united front. I realize that the commitment may be stronger for one parent than for the other, but you both must be able to agree on some common ground rules. It may even be worth writing down a little contract that lists the approach that you can agree on. As a starting point at least get your spouse to read this book.

YOUR PEDIATRICIAN

Your child's doctor should certainly be considered an important member of your support group. You should have already taken your child in for a visit or two and gone over the growth chart. Do not hesitate to make return trips for reassurance or call and ask questions about proper nutrition.

Your pediatrician may serve as a mediator for you and your spouse. I often find that this is a role that I am thrown into when it comes to eating and discipline problems. I offer myself up as the scapegoat; parenting can be a bit easier sometimes when you can say, "Remember Dr. Wilkoff says only two glasses of juice today."

Frequently, I will write down on a prescription pad some dietary guidelines and suggested limits on behavior. This little document can serve as an informal contract that both parents can refer to when a disagreement arises. It may remind Father that snacking in front of his son is undermining his wife's efforts to limit the child's snacks. The contract may also discourage Mother from serving her son a monotonous diet of toasted-cheese sandwiches every night, a practice her husband has been telling her to abandon for months.

Do not be embarrassed to share your intrafamilial differences with the pediatrician. She should be experienced in helping to resolve these conflicts with the welfare of the child in mind. Look on her as an advocate for the child when you as parents are having trouble finding a happy solution. She is the one member of your support group who is accustomed to calls at any hour about anything. Use her.

YOUR DAY CARE PROVIDER

While some day care providers may be part of the problem, they can also be one of your best allies in your struggle to cope. Remember that it is likely that your child will do some of his best eating when he is at day care. The timing is just better. You can ask your provider to keep a record of what your child eats. If you know that your child ate all of his peanut butter and jelly sandwich for lunch and even tried a carrot stick as his afternoon snack, it is very likely to make you feel better as you sit through another evening meal at which your child seems to eat nothing. On the other hand if your day care provider tells you that your child didn't eat any of his vegetable soup at lunch, you may be upset until she tells you that none of the other children did either. It can make you feel much more comfortable about having a picky eater when you realize that you aren't alone. An experienced day care provider has seen scores of children pick their way through meals and can reassure you that your child's behavior is normal.

You could even ask her to videotape a few lunches so that you can enjoy the free-for-all that a communal meal for toddlers can create. As a parent who works out of the home, you are missing out on the fun of watching your child eat, and this, of course, makes watching him not-eat all the more difficult.

If your child is overdrinking or oversnacking, you will need to enlist the help of your day care provider in setting limits. The restrictions on snacks and drinking should be applied to the other children in the day care facility. This should not present a problem because they are part of a good nutritional plan. You may wish to supply written instructions so that you and the day care provider are literally on the same page. She should also give you a written menu for each day so that you can be sure that she is offering a balanced and complete diet.

If your children have an in-home caregiver, you can control what food is being offered. You will still need to make sure that the caregiver sets appropriate limits, and you may need to sit down together and agree on menus for the week. The caregiver may be from a different culture and be unfamiliar with the preparation of the foods your family is accustomed to eating or not-eating, as the case may be. This may not be a problem because your child may develop a liking for ethnic food that he would not have been exposed to until he was an adult. I often hear parents complain/brag that their child will eat unusual and spicy food for the caregiver that they won't touch for them. While children are neophobes for the most part, they can surprise you sometimes when they seem to fall under the magic spell of a caregiver whom they like. It doesn't mean they don't like you. It is sort of a novelty thing.

An experienced day care provider can be an important part of your support team. The best will put her arm around you at the end of your workday and say, "Joshua had some fruit at snack today, and a real good lunch. Don't be surprised if he doesn't eat much for supper" or "He didn't eat all of his lunch today, but don't worry, that big guy shooting baskets in the driveway wasn't much of an eater at this age, either."

Day care can also provide some positive peer pressure. In the festive, although somewhat messy, atmosphere of a group lunch or snack it is likely that your picky eater may temporarily forget his dislike of tuna fish and wolf down his sandwich because everyone else at the table is having such a good time eating theirs. Of course, day care can be a place to learn bad habits, but most of the time children will eat better with their peers at lunch than they will with you later in the day.

YOUR FRIENDS

Parenting in a vacuum can be frightening. That's what friends are for—to fill that lonely void. Share your fears and concerns about your picky eater. Sure, some of your friends will have a little Paul Bunyan who "eats more than his father," but if you talk to enough of your peers, you will hear again and again that picky eating is the norm. Misery loves company, and if you have been miserable watching your child not-eat, share your feelings with a friend.

FORGET THE NUMBERS

I would strongly urge you to avoid counting calories or keeping track of the RDAs (recommended daily allowances) that your child is eating. These numbers are staring you in the face on every packaged food on the shelf. Trying to keep a running tally will make you crazy, and you are crazy to do it. For your numbers to mean anything you would probably have to gather data for at least six months. In doing the research for this book, I learned that the RDAs were developed for the people who need to develop menus for large populations, such as schools and army camps. They were *not* intended to be used for the calculation of an individual's diet. They may be helpful in comparing one food with another, but they certainly are not meant for you to keep tabs on your picky eater.

In addition, I would suggest that you not weigh and measure your child at home. This should be left to your pediatrician. Your measurements may not be as accurate and you will probably do them too frequently to see any meaningful changes. Daily or weekly weights will heighten your concern and your child's anxiety and serve no purpose. In other words *don't do it!*

I would also urge you to avoid weighing and measuring your child's food. As you will see in chapter 18, I have presented the menus in a relatively informal manner, avoiding exact weights and measures when possible. If your child isn't going to eat it anyway, why worry about an "accurate" serving size? Learn to offer your child a token amount of his disliked foods. When you present your child an amount that he has some hope of finishing, he will develop a more positive attitude toward eating. If you do find it necessary at times to weigh or measure food, this should be done out of sight of the child. Remember, you want to be *de*-emphasizing what and how much he is eating. Leave the measurements to the scientists.

WILL HE STARVE OVERNIGHT?

If your child does not eat a big dinner, there should be no concern on your part that "he won't make it through the night" or that "he will wake up hungry at two A.M." You will not be threatening his health by withholding food until the next morning. Remember the research studies in chapter 5 that demonstrated that children know how to balance out their caloric intake. If for some reason your child really did go to bed hungry, he will probably eat a substantial breakfast the next morning and catch up quickly the next day as long as he is offered an adequate menu. It is very important to understand and accept this principle. Later in the book I will offer you suggestions on how to set limits on your child's eating behavior; if you follow them, your child may sometimes go to bed without his dinner. If you are unable to accept the possibility that from time to time your child may go to bed hungry, you are going to have great difficulty in following through with the other suggestions and successfully managing your child's eating behaviors.

PLEASE DON'T WORRY

Just remember:

- If your child was born with a serious medical condition, particularly one involving his digestive system, it would have shown up or been diagnosed by his first birthday.

- Most important, there is substantial scientific evidence that if a small child is provided with an adequate amount of the correct food, he will eventually eat a balanced and healthy diet, even if some of that food, such as corn chips and cookies, might be considered "junk food."

- Children in the toddler age group (two to five years) tend to eat only about one and a half meals per day and usually are done with any significant eating by dinnertime.

- Children come in all shapes and sizes. As long as your child has been examined by his pediatrician and she feels comfortable with his growth chart, you needn't worry.

- Some of us love to eat and some of us just don't. Attempts to make your child into someone with a good appetite is going to be an exercise in frustration.

DO YOU NEED TO CHANGE YOUR

PARENTING STYLE?

How you cope with your child's eating behavior is probably consistent with your general parenting style. In other words if I had watched you and your child at the playground this afternoon, I could probably predict how you would respond to his refusal to eat his peas at dinner this evening. Sociologist Diana Baumrind has described three basic styles in which parents approach their roles and has labeled them *permissive, authoritarian,* and *authoritative.* While you may not feel that your particular style fits exactly into any one of these categories, thinking about this classification should help you understand how you relate to your child.

PERMISSIVE STYLE

As you might expect, the permissive style describes the parent who sets few, if any, limits for his child. I know that some parents avoid making rules because they feel that their child is too young to understand. Other parents seem to trust in some magical power of nature that will allow their child to find the best way to grow up properly if left to his own devices. Limits and rules are regarded as an array of prison bars that will somehow prevent the child from reaching his full potential. Still other parents are afraid of the confrontation that setting and enforcing limits can provoke, often because they lack a safe and rational plan for discipline. Unfortunately, we don't teach child-rearing in school. We are left to figure it out as we go along, relying in large part on our recollection of how our parents did it. When faced with the uncertainty of trying to enforce limits without a clear understanding of how to do it safely, these parents chose to set no limits at all.

AUTHORITARIAN STYLE

At the other pole is the authoritarian style in which the parent seeks to be in total control of the child's behavior. Rules are many and enforcement is strict. Children may be "made" to eat what is good for them. When physical force doesn't seem practical, coercion, trickery, and rewards are employed. The child is presented little opportunity for choice and "must" eat this or that "or else!" (e.g., "Eat your peas or no TV"). Whereas the permissive parent has relinquished control of the situation to the child, the authoritarian parent has kept all the control for himself, leaving the child little room for decision-making.

AUTHORITATIVE STYLE

This is a style of parenting that avoids the excesses of both the permissive and the authoritarian approaches. It is an authoritative style. The two words *authoritarian* and *authoritative* sound so similar, but mean such different things. I have tried to think of another word to replace *authoritative,* but I continue to think it is the best choice for this style of parenting because it still implies that someone has to be in charge. However, the authoritative parent has learned enough about children to set limits within which his child can function safely and still have ample opportunity to make decisions for himself.

Knowledge is at the heart of the authoritative style of parenting. The parent who hopes to create a rational set of limits that will protect the child from the hazards of everyday life learns what those hazards are. With appropriate limits in place, the authoritative parent can then apply a rational set of consequences when his child strays out of bounds.

APPLYING YOUR STYLE

The permissive parent is likely to allow his child to eat and/or drink at will—almost anything, almost anytime. The child is allowed to choose his own menu, and is offered multiple choices if he refuses the meal. High-energy beverages such as juice are always within arm's reach. A permissive parent is very likely to be a short-order cook who fixes each family member his own special diet for every meal, even if this means the child may get cheese sandwiches four times a day.

Some of the consequences of the permissive approach are fairly obvious. If your child is allowed to snack and drink at will he won't be hungry when it comes to scheduled mealtimes. If your child is offered only what he likes, he is likely to eat an unbalanced diet and become malnourished. While young children will regulate their intake safely if presented a nutritionally complete diet that includes a broad variety, they can't be trusted to do so if the proper variety is not offered. A permissive parent is likely to lack the discipline to offer only a healthful diet, particularly if his child has rejected these foods at an early age.

A permissive parent is also likely to tolerate chaos at the dinner table. If your child is allowed an unrestricted range of behavior while eating, the dining room may rapidly take on the appearance of the dining hall in the movie *Animal House*—not a pretty sight. I remember a mother telling me that she allowed her child to ride his tricycle around the dinner table because it was the only way he would eat anything. I can only imagine how unpleasant it must have been to eat a meal with the sound of screeching tires ringing in one's ears.

Many children raised in permissive households are allowed to get up and down from the table at will. At our children's birthday parties, we could easily see which children had been free to roam from the table in their own homes. Even the other children found it distracting and would chastise their wandering peers for interfering with the celebration. A young child without some guidance is likely to create a dining atmosphere few adults would find pleasurable. Hopes of table manners in the future of a child raised in the permissive style would seem dim.

There also can be some unfortunate consequences when the authoritarian style is applied to feeding children. These include a tense, adversarial atmosphere at meals, bellyaches, and even vomiting, to name just a few. Instead of a blessing or toast, the meal might start with an admonition: "Now remember, Daniel, last night you didn't eat any vegetables. Tonight you had better clean your plate or you are going to bed a half hour early." Things usually go downhill from there, with little conversation about anything other than eating habits as the rest of the family watches every mouthful little Daniel does or doesn't take. They hope that tonight Daniel will clean his plate and avoid another tearful tantrum and dinner-ending scene.

One of the most important drawbacks of the authoritarian style is that a child who has been given little opportunity for choice when younger will be less likely to develop good decision-making skills as she gets older. If your child has always had to do it Daddy's or Mommy's way, she will be in a real pickle when she begins to spend time away from home. As the years go by, Daddy or Mommy won't always be around to "help" with those hard choices. Some of these choices will be about what to eat and will need to be made for herself when she is by herself. Dr. Susan Johnson of the Center for Human Nutrition of the University of Colorado Health Science Center has said that the "excessive vigilance" that some controlling parents maintain over their daughters' diets is "probably related to why you see a much higher incidence of eating disorders in girls at a later age." Decision-making is a skill that is learned with practice. The controlling or authoritarian style of parenting leaves little opportunity for this learning to take place.

An authoritative parent will present his family with a well-balanced menu that his child is physically capable of eating. The portions are appropriately sized, and each food is cut to a size and is of a texture that the child can easily chew and swallow. Limits on snacks and beverages are clearly defined as to amount and timing, and a system of rational consequences (sometimes known as discipline) is in place should the child test the limits. For example, if the child has decided to not-eat and is repeatedly poking his sister, he would be sent to his room until the meal is over. He is told to leave the table not because he was not-eating but because he was ruining the meal for the rest of the family. There are no bribes for eating lima beans and desserts are served without condition. The eating habits of family members are not topics for discussion at the table. Some people at the table clean their plates, some don't, but never is heard a discouraging word. Conversation ranges from the weather to the fireman's visit to nursery school. Mealtimes for the authoritative family are enjoyable times, free of pressure and tension.

Do you see yourself or your spouse yet? You may be having trouble accepting that you are either a permissive or authoritarian parent because I have purposely drawn them in their extremes. But be honest, don't you fit somewhere? Which way do you lean? Do you tend to be more permissive or authoritarian? It is possible that you are on the permissive side of things, and your spouse is more authoritarian. Obviously, this arrangement is going to result in conflict when it comes to mealtimes. You may be busy preparing the third attempt at an acceptable meal while your spouse has just delivered an ultimatum that your child finish everything on his plate or there is no video before bed. Or your spouse may have been allowing the child to keep his "wander bottle" and you don't think it's a good idea. The mixed message presented by these conflicting styles can be very unsettling to your child. Some children will take advantage of this chink in your parental armor and exploit it by playing you off one another. There are other children who will become depressed when they realize their parents can't get their act together. The bottom line is that when your child is faced with such opposite approaches, he will not know which to believe and might end up following neither one.

I hope that this book can serve as a guide that each of you can refer to and that you can agree on a united approach to your child's eating. If your approaches conflict, agree to open the book and see what Dr. Wilkoff has to say. I can't guarantee that I always provide the best answer, but it should be one that you both can accept. It should make it easier for you and your child.

You may even want to sit down together and write out a little contract with each other. It can spell out what each of you agrees to say or not say, eat or not eat. This sort of postnuptial agreement can prevent arguments and speed the resolution of many of the differences that are interfering with your management of your child's picky eating.

- We agree not to snack or drink soft drinks in front of Zachary.
- We agree to only one menu per meal.
- We agree not to discuss Zachary's eating habits at the dinner table.
- We agree to limit Zachary's juice intake to two cups per day.

Signed

_____

John Doe

_____

Mary Doe

_____

Date

PARENTING SCHIZOPHRENIA

It may be that you as an individual are employing a mixture of authoritarian and permissive styles of parenting when it comes to your child's eating. For example, you may be permissive when it comes to drinking or snacks by allowing him to have juice any time he says he is thirsty, or allowing a slice of cheese whenever he is hungry. However, when meals come around you may do an about-face and take on an authoritarian tone and order your child to finish his vegetables or there will be no bedtime story. Or you may exert strict control over your child's snacks by limiting him to two graham crackers in the morning and one carrot stick in the afternoon and then fix him pasta every night for dinner because you know he won't touch anything else. This sort of parental schizophrenia is counterproductive. If you allow your child to eat and/or drink his fill during the day, you can't expect him to have any appetite when mealtimes come around. Consistency is an important quality for parents to display. Children understand it and are comforted when they see it in adults they want to love and respect. Despite what you may feel sometimes, children are good listeners. They are literal in their interpretation and quick to point out the inconsistencies in both what you say and what you do.

WE ALL GET TIRED

Sometimes you start off the day with "good" intentions and try to be authoritarian and stick to the rules, but as the day wears on, you just get too tired. You decide to take the path of least resistance and your parenting style becomes permissive. This can happen to the best of us. Fatigue is not the only reason that parents become inconsistent in their approach to their children's behavior, but it is the most common. Job responsibilities, pressure from grandparents and friends, can distract even the most committed parents from carrying out their best intentions of setting appropriate limits and sticking to them, but I have found it is fatigue that most parents complain about. Parenting is hard work and to do a good job you must be well rested. By budgeting enough time for yourself during the day, you will find that by evening you still have enough emotional stamina to resist the temptation to be either permissive or short-tempered and authoritarian. If you work outside the home and have allowed yourself to become so overcommitted that you don't even have time to sit down for lunch and take a little stroll outside, you are jeopardizing your chances of becoming a parent who can make rational choices and cope with the challenges of a picky eater. Many of the parents that I work with are so exhausted at the end of the day that they are incapable of effective parenting, and we often must start with helping them to reprioritize their days to allow enough time and energy for parenting in the critical late afternoon and evening hours.

BECOMING AN AUTHORITATIVE PARENT

The answer is simple. First, you need to learn enough about what normal children are about so that you can confidently set rational limits for your child. When it comes to eating habits, this book is your resource. For information on the broader topic of child behavior, you may want to take a course in parenting, read a variety of books, and talk to your pediatrician about specific aspects of your child's behavior that puzzle you. The limits that you set should be broad enough to allow your child to make some decisions for himself but crafted in such a way as to guarantee that he can grow up safely. For example, tethering your two-year-old to a stake in the backyard with a ten-foot rope may be safe enough, but it gives him little room for exploration. However, if you live on a busy street, allowing him to run free is unacceptable. A fence on the perimeter of the yard would give him room to ramble but protect him from being struck by an automobile.

You must have an effective discipline plan, which you can employ if the limits are challenged. Merely screaming, "Don't do that, Michelle!" in a louder and louder voice is going to do little to deter little Michelle from picking the leaves off your African violet. There needs to be another phrase, which begins, "And if you do it again . . ." In other words there must be a consequence for behavior that exceeds the limits.

Finally, you must be flexible in both setting limits and applying discipline. This flexibility means that you have some understanding of your child as a person and acknowledge that each day is different. You must be aware that children are always in a state of transition. They are growing and developing and so demand an approach that is flexible enough to keep up with these transitions. The limits and expectations that you have for a two-year-old will not be appropriate for a four-year-old. The older child should be able to remain seated for a meal that lasts for half an hour, while the younger one shouldn't be expected to be entertained by the event for more than fifteen minutes. You must understand your own child well enough to know how he will respond in different situations. You must accept that while in many ways your child is like all other two-year-olds, he is also unique, and the limits your neighbor sets for his child might not be appropriate for yours. For example, some children are by nature more adventuresome and will test the boundaries of their environment daily. Others are more content to stay put. Your three-year-old may be happy to sit for half an hour in one spot building a fort, while your nephew of the same age is eager for a change in activity every ten or fifteen minutes and would prefer to find out what is under every piece of furniture and in the back of each closet in the house. While many of us would rather parent your child because he is easier to manage, your nephew's behavior is also age-appropriate, and his curiosity may eventually be channeled into a research project that wins a Nobel prize. You need to know where your child fits on this spectrum if you are going to set enforceable limits that will allow adequate opportunity for decision-making. If you were to ask your nephew to sit on the couch for ten minutes while you were wrapping a package, you would find yourself reminding him several times to get back on the couch. Your expectations for that child in that situation are unreasonable. Your own child might be able to hold out for the whole ten minutes. That doesn't mean he is any better than his cousin, just different.

The authoritative parent also has a safe, rational, and effective discipline plan that can be employed if and when the child crosses the boundaries that have been set. Corporal punishment is dangerous because it has a very narrow margin of safety. Most parents will fortunately err on the gentler side, and find that their child seems unfazed by the paddling. Striking any harder runs perilously close to abuse, and suggests to the child that when he is angry enough, it is all right to hit. Sitting down and talking about the situation may make some of us feel that we have done something, but this method is ineffective. The method known most commonly as "time-out" is the most effective and safest way of enforcing limits and will be described in chapter 10 as it applies to eating behavior.

With this knowledge about your child and informed expectations about children in general, you as an authoritative parent can create a set of limits that will allow your child enough freedom to make some decisions on his own and still avoid the hazards inherent in everyday life.

With knowledge comes confidence. Most *authoritarian* parents probably struggle for control over their child's behavior because they lack confidence in their child to make correct decisions. They are afraid to leave any room for error. On the other hand, as an *authoritative* parent, you will want to learn enough about your own child to have educated expectations about his normal growth and development. This will allow you the confidence to relinquish some control to your child. You should also understand enough about children to realize that if you allow your child to set the limits, then chaos is inevitable.

When it comes to nutrition, this means that you must learn how to offer menus that are nutritionally complete and balanced. You also must have a good understanding about how young children grow and have reasonable expectations about how children eat when offered a healthy diet. You also must understand the consequences of behaviors such as overdrinking and snacking on foods high in sugar or fat content.

You will learn that a normal child can be trusted to eat a healthy diet, if a broad and varied diet is offered. With the help of your pediatrician, you can reassure yourself that your child is healthy. You must learn what constitutes a nutritious diet and how to present it in an atmosphere that is conducive to healthy eating habits. Chapters 14 and 16 will answer these questions. With this knowledge you should become more relaxed about your child's behavior patterns when it comes to food. You should be able to set limits on his eating that make sense scientifically and still leave him room enough to make his own decisions. Finally, you must develop a discipline strategy that can be applied when your limits are challenged.

With this foundation you can build a style of parenting that allows your child to make safe choices within a set of boundaries that are not imposed heavy-handedly. But first you will make some rules.

EVERYONE NEEDS SOME RULES

It would be nice if coping with your picky eater could simply consist of presenting him a balanced meal in a pleasant setting and then sitting back and watching worry-free. I wish that raising children were that easy. While they may not be terribly adventuresome in trying new foods, children are by nature going to explore their environment to its boundaries. Some engineering types might describe it as "pushing the envelope." My mother would have described it as "looking for trouble." To be a successful parent, you must become skilled at defining and then patrolling these boundaries. This is currently called "setting limits."

For several generations the issue of discipline had received little attention by the so-called experts who advised parents on child-rearing. However, it has become obvious that the failure to have some rules (or *limits,* if you prefer) for children can result in a chaos that is both unpleasant in the short term and that leaves them poorly prepared for the realities of life in the long run.

The first problem is choosing limits that make sense and are age-appropriate. If the rules are unreasonably restrictive, they will ignite constant conflict and be unenforceable. The definition of these limits is an art that must take into account the child's personality, his developmental stage, and focus clearly on the problem at hand. It would be foolish to apply the same limits to an inquisitive two-year-old that you might feel are appropriate for a more insightful five-year-old. The second problem is how to respond when the limits are breached. A thorough discussion of the broad topic of discipline (limit-setting) is beyond the scope of this little book, and I will limit my suggested rules to those that concern eating. However, I will recommend some consequences that may be applied to other disciplinary issues. Some of these rules have already been introduced in other chapters and their discussion here should serve as a review and a reemphasis.

Since the child is going to be the target of most of these limits, it seems only fair to start off with some rules aimed at his parents, and that means *you!*

RULES FOR PARENTS

1. EATING IS NOT TO BE DISCUSSED AT OR NEAR MEALTIME.

In fact, until you feel comfortable that your concerns about your child's picky eating are under control, it would be best not to raise the issue while the child is in earshot. This means that you should not cajole, bribe, threaten, chide about his eating at the dinner table, nor in the hours before the meal has started. If you feel it is necessary to discuss some of the rules with your child, this should be done at a time distant from a meal. This discussion should not be a lecture about the value of a good diet, but merely a review of the rules if there have been some problems.

Again, these little talks should be kept to a minimum. Your child is not stupid; he heard you the first time. Remember, your actions speak louder than words. Your ability to set and maintain the limits will go much farther than a lot of hot air.

This admonition includes positive comments about other family members' eating habits. "Robbie [older brother] is really eating his broccoli well tonight. I guess he'll grow up big and strong" is not something that needs to be pointed out. The picky eater has eyes; he just doesn't have an appetite. A comment such as "The sweet potatoes are extra good, Margie" is harmless, as long as it isn't followed by "Why don't you try them, Josh?"

This rule can be extremely difficult to follow. It is hard to bite your tongue and eat a meal at the same time. It is also very tempting to share your worries with friends. Remember, children can hear better than you think. If you want to commiserate with other parents of picky eaters, do it at adults-only functions.

2. MEALTIME CONVERSATION SHOULD BE POSITIVE.

Dinnertime is not the opportunity to confront an older sister about her problems with doing homework, nor is it a time to launch a tirade about what a jerk your boss has been. It is perfectly fine to share some of the problems you have experienced at work, but when it takes on the tone of whining or a harangue, it ruins everyone else's appetite, particularly the picky eater's. There is plenty to talk about at mealtime without creating an unpleasant atmosphere on the one hand or sounding sappy sweet on the other. If you are having trouble thinking of something, ask the children about their day.

3. LIMIT MEALS TO TWENTY MINUTES IN LENGTH.

If your child is going to eat something, it is going to occur in the first twenty minutes. There is nothing to be gained by forcing your child to stay at the table until he has cleaned his plate or simply eaten anything. If you are fast eaters and finish in ten minutes, learn to slow down so that you won't be sitting around for ten minutes watching your child not-eat. That wait will try your patience and you will be tempted to break the rule about mentioning your child's eating habits during the meal. If everyone is having a good time, whether they are eating or not, of course there is no reason to limit the length of the meal. However, the picky eater can leave the table when he is done eating.

4. STICK TO YOUR PLANNED MENU.

This is another way of saying that you won't fix your child something off the menu just so you can watch him eat. Mothers seem to have the most trouble with this rule, but it is a very important one. Fixing that cheese sandwich for the child who doesn't eat his pork chop and broccoli is not coping, it's copping out. Plan your menu in advance and then stick to your guns. Remember, this is not Alice's Restaurant.

5. FOLLOW THE SAME SNACKING RULES YOU HAVE MADE FOR YOUR CHILD.

If you are going to set limits for your child, you must observe them yourself. It is unfair to snack in front of your child when he is being told that he must adhere to a schedule. Everyone's snacks should consist of healthful foods, not just your child's. This means fruit instead of salty snacks such as potato chips; and fresh vegetables such as raw carrots and cucumber spears replace high-energy foods like cookies and candy, which often have an excess of fat and sugar. Choosing low-fat ice cream for a snack misses the point. While it may be better than full-fat ice cream, it is still an inappropriate snack when compared with something more nutritious. This would seem to be an obvious statement, but I am afraid that I continue to encounter many parents who were thoughtless about their eating behavior around their children. The parent who is at home with the child should make his or her snacks coincident with the child's, or have them while the child is napping or out of the house.

6. SERVE APPROPRIATELY SIZED PORTIONS OF BOTH FAVORED AND UNFAVORED FOODS.

Yes, we can trust children to balance their diet over the long haul, but I think that it is reasonable to impose a little balancing act yourself on a daily basis. Don't present overly large portions of foods that you know the child is not going to eat or he has never tried before. If you are going to tell your child that he can't have seconds on his favorite foods until he has cleaned his plate (see Rule 4 later in this chapter), it is unfair and counterproductive to give him anything more than a token serving of the foods he dislikes. An example of the application of this rule might be a meal of macaroni and cheese and peas. Your child loves macaroni and cheese but won't touch his peas. Give him a generous portion of macaroni and cheese and a token serving of peas; a teaspoon would be a good place to start. By keeping the portion of the new or disliked food small, you are increasing the chances that he will try to eat and finish it in an effort to have more of his favorite.

IT'S A FAMILY AFFAIR

You know that coping with your picky eater may require some changes in your own eating habits. If you have been snacking on whatever you like whenever you like, this will have to stop. But you are an adult and a parent and this kind of sacrifice is one you should make willingly because the well-being of your child is at stake. However, if you have other children who are not picky eaters, you will probably have trouble convincing them to follow the same rules that you have set for their overly selective sibling.

"Why can't I have two glasses of juice now? I'm not the one who won't finish his peas tonight. Mom, can't I have some peanut butter crackers? I'm a growing twelve-year-old. When was the last time I didn't clean my plate?" These are just some of the arguments you are likely to hear from your children with robust appetites when you try to enforce the limitations that I have suggested for your picky eater, particularly if one of your children is an adolescent male.

It is the same old story. You have to make rules for everyone because one segment of the population can't be counted on to discipline themselves. Remember when the whole class had to stay in from recess because one classmate was throwing spit-balls? It just didn't seem fair.

I don't think that there is an easy solution, but there are some strategies that you can try to minimize the intrafamilial friction created by your picky eater. First, you can take the hearty eaters aside and explain to them that while they don't have a problem, their sibling does, and that the entire family must participate in the remedy. Describe the changes that you are trying to make in your parenting style and how difficult it has been. Tell the omnivores you will always provide them with healthy food in more than adequate amounts, but that you are going to set some limits on the timing and the choices.

Remind them that some of their requests for more food are unhealthy, but reassure them that you won't let them go hungry. Following the rules you have set for their picky sibling will help them to refine their own healthy eating habits. Tell the appetite-advantaged children that you can occasionally bend the rules for them, but they must be careful to have these extra snacks out of sight and earshot of the picky eater.

Tell the other children that one of the most important, but

difficult, parts of coping with a picky eater involves not talking about eating styles at mealtimes. Suggest that their failure to observe this code of silence may meet with disciplinary action if it persists.

Occasionally, it is the younger sibling who is the better eater. Sometimes so young that it would be fruitless to enter into a rational discussion about enforcing limitations. In these cases it is the picky eater who must understand that his younger sibling eats well and that this fact allows you to be a bit more flexible from time to time. However, in general it is best to create a set of limitations that can be applied safely to the entire family, and then stick to them. The adjustment may take a few weeks, but once you get the whole family on the same page, coping with the picky eater will become much easier.

RULES FOR CHILDREN

1. ALL EATING AND DRINKING IS TO BE DONE AT THE TABLE OR IN A HIGH CHAIR.

There are several rationales for this rule. First, it can act as a deterrent to uncontrolled snacking and drinking. These two excesses can contribute to poor eating at mealtimes, as well as obesity. Limiting them to the table can serve as a reminder to both parent and child that there is a time and a place for everything. Second, by returning eating to the table, you are making a good first step toward emphasizing its social side. If you are going to rebuild meals into enjoyable family events, you must first get everyone to the table.

For the child between the ages of one and two, it may be necessary to physically restrain him in his high chair until he gets the message. This should not be viewed as binding the child so that you can force food down his throat. This young child often is so boisterous and has such short attention spans that you may need to put a harness on him just to keep him in the chair for five or ten minutes, to give his appetite a chance. Some of you may find the notion of tying a child into a chair for his meals abhorrent and reminiscent of the atrocities we hear about in Third World orphanages. But using a restraint such as a harness tethered to the back of the high chair is much better than you hopping up every few seconds to jam him back in his seat with the accompanying yelling and screaming (his and yours). The alternative is to have the child standing up at his whim, spilling food and drink all over the place or sliding out under the tray and escaping from the dining area. A firm mechanical restraint will give the child few choices to do the wrong thing and he will usually calm down and behave. He may or may not eat, but remember that's okay. If after ten minutes it is clear that he is not going to eat and will just make a fuss, take him out of the harness and let him down. The meal is over, at least for him. Remember, I am advocating this practice only up to about age two, and it is not being done so that you can force-feed your child. You are only providing a simple mechanical reminder to stay seated at the table for a few minutes. I hope that if your child has a problem staying seated that you can bring yourself to use a harness in this fashion. You will find that usually you will only need to do it for a few weeks until things settle down. It really isn't barbaric, it's merely pragmatic.

2. LIMIT DRINKS.

All drinking should be done from a cup and in the high chair or at the table. The amount and types of permissible drinks are:

One four-ounce cup of milk at each meal.

One four-ounce cup of juice at each of two snacks.

Unlimited water.

3. TWO AND ONLY TWO SNACKS PER DAY.

The picky eater should be offered two nutritious snacks at specific times, one midmorning and one midafternoon. Fruits and vegetables are preferred, but baked goods that are not high in sugar, salt, or fat content are acceptable (see chapter 13 for specific amounts and suggested foods). These snacks should be in close association to some activity that the child can understand, such as a nap, activity, or TV show. The most important reason to have these snacks at specific times is to aid you in your efforts at setting limits. It is likely that your child is going to challenge you by begging for snacks off the schedule. With a firm and predictable snack routine in place, you will be able to discipline the child for whining or begging for the extra snack. It will be easier to say, "You know that you will have a snack after *Mr. Rogers' Neighborhood;* if you keep bugging me about it, you will have to go to your room."

Remember, all snacks should be eaten at the table, to keep that association strong, and keep your floors in the rest of the house clean.

4. NO SECONDS UNLESS HE HAS CLEANED HIS PLATE.

This is *not* to be misinterpreted as an invitation to join the old "clean plate club" that you and I may have been inducted into. It is a way to prevent your child from overdoing on one food to the exclusion of others on any one day. Yes, I will readily admit that this rule may be a bit at odds with the observation that foods eaten to gain reward are likely to be less preferred when the reward is removed. However, this should not be presented as a reward, but merely a family rule that everyone observes. In a way it is more of a manners issue. If you have truly been generous in serving the preferred food, this issue is much less likely to come up.

5. THE CHILD DOES NOT HAVE TO
STAY AT THE TABLE IF HE IS DONE EATING.

With the exception of the one- or two-year-old described in Rule 1, the child may choose to get down from the table when he has finished eating. By age three you can expect him to be polite and ask to be excused, but this request should be granted with little if any comment on your part. As time goes on, you ought to be successful in creating an enjoyable atmosphere at the table so that the child will want to stay seated even though he doesn't feel like eating.

It should be made clear, however, that the meal will be eaten in one sitting. If anyone gets down from the table for any frivolous reason, they do not return to the table. This, we would hope, will prevent the annoying behavior of a child bouncing up and down from floor to table. There is one important exception to this rule. There is a little habit that all of us have called the gastrocolic reflex. When our stomach begins to fill, there is a reflex wave of peristalsis that goes down our intestines. When it reaches the large bowel, there may be an urge to have a bowel movement. This reflex is very active in small babies, and it is why they seem to always have a bowel movement while you are feeding them. It can still be quite vigorous in small children and it is not unusual for some children to have to excuse themselves from the table to have a bowel movement shortly after they have started. If they tend to constipation, they may have pain as these waves occur when they really should be having a bowel movement. Understanding this bit of gastrointestinal physiology may help you to be a bit more understanding of the child who has to regularly excuse himself from the table to have a bowel movement. As unpleasant as it may be for the parent who may have to assist the child in wiping his bottom, there isn't much to do about the problem. A small snack an hour before the meal may help, but of course this may blunt the child's appetite for the meal.

6. BEHAVIOR IN THE DINING AREA
SHOULD NOT BE DISRUPTIVE.

The child may get down from the table and play quietly in the same room, and even participate in the conversation, but if his behavior becomes unruly either at the table or in the dining area then he is sent to his room until the meal is over. Make it clear that this banishment is *not* because he was not eating, but because his behavior was disruptive to those who were trying to have a nice meal.

Remember that we have agreed that you weren't going to discuss who was eating what and when and this situation is a good test of your resolve. Your emphasis is on creating a pleasant dining atmosphere in which the family members can eat or not-eat as they choose. If your child has chosen to not-eat, but is willing to share in the ambience, he can do so, even if he has decided to get down from the table. However, if he decides to misbehave or demands negative attention, then he should be taken to his room for a "time-out" until the meal has ended. Of course, in the short term this tactic may seem counterproductive because the process of taking the child to his room and time in his room may be accompanied by rather noisy objections. However, this response should be temporary and not persist for more than several similar episodes—until the child understands that the limits are reasonable and will be enforced. These unpleasant meals should be looked on as an investment for the long term. Remember, you were probably having unpleasant meals before, but now you have a plan with a clear and reasonable end point.

WHEN THE RULES

ARE CHALLENGED

You have set some limits. You have promised to follow your own rules. Now what are you going to do when your child steps out of bounds? It is time to face the issue of enforcement. There continues to be debate among some pediatricians about the value of physical discipline (e.g., spanking). However, I suspect that the vast majority of pediatricians and other experts in child-rearing would join me in saying that there is very little, if any, place for tactics such as spanking. While physical discipline may be effective in certain situations, it has a very narrow safety margin. Try to answer the question "How hard do you spank a three-year-old?" Most parents hit so gently that the child just laughs it off, but there is a fine line between physical discipline and child abuse. The answer is to avoid spanking, particularly when it comes to issues surrounding your child's eating habits.

MAKING TIME-OUT WORK

The safest and most effective means of enforcing the limits you have set is commonly known as time-out. You are probably familiar with the term and the technique but like many of the parents in my practice may have found that it doesn't work for your child. Every week I sit down with parents who are at the end of their ropes because they have yet to find an effective means of enforcing their rules. I ask if they have tried time-out and they answer yes, but it hasn't worked. I then ask them to describe how exactly they administer the method. "Well, we sit him in a chair, but he won't stay there unless one of us stands right there and watches him." I then ask if they have tried putting the child in his room, and they answer, "Oh, yes, but he keeps coming out" or "When the three minutes are up, he is still screaming." If you can hear yourself giving these answers, then you haven't really been doing time-out.

Let me say right up front that if your young child will sit quietly in a chair for three or four minutes without you standing right there, he probably didn't need the discipline. A child who is that compliant could probably have been managed with a few stern words. If you are going to do time-out, the child should be sent (more likely taken) to his room. This is particularly true for misbehavior at the dinner table when it is important to remove the child from the eating environment. The important aspect of time-out is separation of the child from the warm center of family life. Many parents will object, "I don't want my child to view his room as a prison." Not to worry, your child is not stupid. He will quickly realize that it is less important where he is sent and more important what he is being excluded from. My wife and I have used their bedrooms for time-out for all of our children, and they continue to view their rooms as their special place and enjoy going there on their own. In addition, often a child is misbehaving because he is overtired. The child who is sent to his room may very likely cry himself to sleep and get some much-needed rest.

When the child is in his room, the door acts as a good sound buffer so that the rest of us trying to enjoy our meal don't have to listen to the full force of the child's complaints. More important, the physical separation can act as an important safety feature. If you have reached the end of your rope, you will be less likely to react by striking your child in anger. The time-out can function well for a cooling-off period for you as well as an enforcement technique for the child. (Be honest. Sometimes when you're tired the friction between you and your child is as much your fault as his.)

If time-out is going to be effective, the child must stay in his room for a specified period of time. Many children will accept the closed door as a barrier. However, some children will simply open the door and come out, rendering the time-out ineffective. The obvious and appropriate response is to latch the door closed. Simple as this step may sound, it is amazing to me how many parents aren't willing to make the trip to the hardware store and spend the $1.99 for a little hook and eye to install. I guess you may be afraid that word will get out around the neighborhood that you lock your child in his room. Please don't worry about it. The buck has to stop somewhere, and a little piece of hardware can do it so easily. You will find that you really won't have to use it but a few times. The mere existence of the latch is a reminder that you are serious about enforcing the limits you have set.

How long should the child stay in his room? There is a rule of thumb that says, "One minute per year of age," which seems to work pretty well. The next question is "When do you start counting?" I think the answer is "When you hear quiet coming from the room." You tell the child that you will start the kitchen timer when you hear silence, and when the timer dings, the child can come out. Sometimes the child is so upset that you may want to shorten the whole process by going into the room when it becomes obvious that the screaming is going to go on for a long time. You then cuddle and hold the child and help him calm down. You tell him that now that he is quiet you are going to leave and start the timer for two or three minutes, and that's it.

When the child is in his room for time-out, his door should be treated as a soundproof barrier that admits only silence. You behave as though you don't hear his rantings. You don't answer his questions nor do you offer any suggestions. When you hear silence you start the timer. This rule of thumb should prevent the senseless yelling contests that so often prolong the ordeal and can make time-out ineffective.

When the child has "served his time," he comes out and is greeted by a big hug and a kiss as he is welcomed back into the family circle. It is pointless to sit the child down to rehash the incident in hopes of avoiding confrontation in the future. Your child is smart enough to know why he was sent to his room without hearing it again. After the time-out has been completed, the crime is forgiven, and you reemphasize how nice it is to be part of the family again with a warm and caring physical sign of affection.

WHEN TO USE TIME-OUT

Now that you have learned some sensible rules that can be used to help mold your child's eating behavior, and you have learned a safe and powerful tool for enforcing these rules, it's time to run through a few examples.

- Your child is begging for his third cup of juice of the day. You might say, "You know that you have already had your snacks with juice today. If you are thirsty, you can sit in your high chair and have some water." If the child keeps hounding you, you then say, "If you ask me one more time for juice, I am going to send you to your room." He asks again and, bingo, it's off to his room.

- It is eight-thirty in the morning. Your child has already had breakfast and he is begging for a snack. You say, "You know that we'll have snack at ten, that's just before Mr. Rogers comes on the TV. If you keep bugging me, you will have to go to your room." Another whine for a cracker and it's off to time-out.

  You will notice there are no second or third chances; there is one warning and a prompt response. For everyone's sake there is no sense in dragging this out.

- It's dinnertime. Your child has announced for the third time he is not eating anything that is on his plate. You then ask, "If you are done eating, you can get down from the table and play here in the dining room quietly." He gets down eagerly but begins to whine that he wants to sit in your lap. Your response could be, "We are still eating. I'll be glad to sit with you after dinner and read a story, but if you keep on whining, you will have to go to your room until the meal is over." Another whine and you send him off to his room until you are done eating. Here is an example of when you might extend the time-out beyond the "one minute per year of age" guideline. However, this can be negotiated, depending on the specifics of the situation.

The limits you choose to set and the exact manner in which you are going to administer time-out should be discussed with the child at a quiet time not related to meals. They do not need to be hammered in. Your actions are going to speak louder than your words. You are going to issue simple warnings that can be understood and that involve threats you can easily carry out (i.e., time-out). There are going to be no second chances, and any yelling and screaming will be from the child, not you. It sounds easy and sensible now, but in the heat of the battle, it can be very difficult. Try to remain calm. If carried out well, you will find that issues of limits and enforcement fade into the background very quickly and you can begin to enjoy meals again.

BRIBERY WILL GET YOU NOWHERE

You may be tempted to resort to bribery when your picky eater has rejected his lima beans for the twentieth time. Some of your friends who dabble in psychology may have even suggested that you try "positive reinforcement." They may have told you how to make a chart on the refrigerator on which your child can post stickers he has earned for cleaning his plate or eating spoonfuls of peas.

While this behavior management technique may be effective for such things as toilet training and for discouraging some misbehaviors such as whining or leaving toys out, it really has no place in dealing with a picky eater. Although bribery may sometimes encourage a child to eat one more mouthful of broccoli, its effectiveness is short-lived. Studies have shown that in the long run this kind of positive reinforcement does not result in change in the child's preference, and in fact may result in backlash in which the child will shun the food when the reward is withdrawn.

Your child already knows that if he eats well, it will make you happy. Even if you don't say a word, your body language will tell him that you were pleased by the way he finished his supper. There is no need to create a special reward system for eating what you have presented. Call it positive reinforcement or bribery, it has no place in the plan for coping with your picky eater.

SETTING AN EXAMPLE

Even if you adopt a style that is neither too permissive nor too heavy-handed, there is still at least one major pitfall of parenting you must avoid. You may say all the right things, set all the right limits, and employ rational consequences with the wisdom of Solomon. However, if you don't set a good example, your success as a parent is likely to be doomed to failure.

"Do as I say, not as I do." We can't really call it an old adage, it is really an old joke. We all know that whether we are children or adults we are going to ultimately judge others for what they do and not what they say. As children we are likely to follow the example of our parents' actions. Children are more likely to smoke if their parents smoke, and parents who are picky eaters are more likely to have children with similar attitudes toward food.

As a parent you are your child's first and most important role model. It is a heavy responsibility and must be taken seriously. If there are certain foods that you dislike, keep it to yourself. This doesn't mean that you have to choke down a huge bowel of lima beans just to set a good example, but it does mean that "if you can't say anything nice, don't say anything at all." The things you say about food can shape the way in which your child approaches the meals that are presented to him. If your three-year-old already knows your ten least favorite foods, you have been sharing more about yourself than he needs to know. In fact, if he knows that there is anything that you "absolutely won't [not can't] eat," you are contributing to his tendency to be picky. Your negative attitudes about certain foods can validate and reinforce his refusal to try new and less-favored foods. Your picky ways are not something you want to advertise or have your child emulate.

You need to be a good sport when your spouse asks for something on your disfavored list. Unless you have a doctor's note confirming an allergy, you should ask for a small (token) portion and give it a try. Your willingness to be adventuresome in your approach to food will set a good example for the little neophobes in the family. Your picky eater should be served a broad variety of foods, and that means you will be served them as well. It doesn't mean that you *have* to eat them, just as your child doesn't have to eat them, but if you take your role as a parent seriously, you will give some new foods a try. Maybe some of your own picky eating will resolve itself if you would just be a bit more adventuresome.

There are several ways that you can broaden your family's repertoire of menus. First, avoid having a monotonous rotation in which each night of the week has a predictable menu. While many of us feel more secure with routines that can make meal-planning less of a challenge, the habit of having spaghetti every Wednesday night, meat loaf on Thursday, and pizza on Friday is not helping your picky eater gain more experience with different foods. Once every week or two you might consider having a "theme" meal in which the menu is representative of a nation or ethnic group. These meals could be eaten at restaurants, taken out, or prepared at home. You could also have an occasional buffet or smorgasbord at home in which there is a broad variety of foods presented, some that maybe you have not tried before. Make it obvious that you are enjoying trying different foods, separately and in combination. Your picky eater may stay on the sidelines the first few times, but he will be watching and will see how much fun you are having venturing into the unknown.

You can also broaden your menus by building on family preferences. If spaghetti with tomato sauce is everyone's favorite, try a different pasta shape with the same sauce, or the same spaghetti with a different sauce. It won't work every time, but it is a step in the right direction. Make sure that you keep your comments positive, even if the experiment is a failure. Nothing ventured, nothing gained.

If you are going to set limits on drinking and snacking for your child, those limits must apply to you as well. If you are in the habit of reaching in to the refrigerator for a bottle of soft drink whenever you wish, how can you tell your child that he only gets two cups of juice a day? If you sit down with a bag of chips late in the afternoon, what happens to your credibility when you tell your child that he only gets some apple slices and a handful of raisins at three-thirty? When you bring the evening newspaper to the dinner table, think of the message that you are giving your child about the shared experiences that can take place during a family meal. Show your child that sitting down at the table isn't just about eating. It is a time to talk to one another and not to read a magazine or watch the evening news.

You can read this book from front to back and then pick it up and do it again, but you will never be able to successfully parent your child, picky eater or not, unless you are a living example of the principles that you wish your child to adopt. Your role as a parent is to first of all set an example, a good example.

IF YOU PUSH

If you are going to cope successfully with your child's picky eating, you must abandon any efforts at emotional arm-twisting. Your new role is to present your child with an adequate diet in pleasant surroundings and then to do nothing extraordinary to get him to eat it. This means no direct confrontation, bribery, coercion, or trying to make your child feel guilty for not-eating.

You may have begun using these tactics without realizing it. Have you threatened, "There is no TV unless you finish your vegetables"? Have you pleaded, "If you eat one spoonful of peas, you can have ice cream for dessert"? Have you whined, "I spent an hour out of a very busy day fixing this meal and you haven't even taken a bite"? Have you ever said, "You are never going to be big enough to play football if you don't finish everything on your plate"?

We have all slipped into one or more of these strategies when our child was not-eating, and we have heard them from our parents when we were being picky. They are so common that one might consider them clichés. Begin to listen to yourself as you talk to your child about his eating habits. Think about how your child may interpret your words. Does it just boil down to a power struggle with food as one of the weapons? Is there some special relationship between eating and the privilege of watching television? Do you want your child to think of eating as a job that allows him to earn TV time or desserts? No, your child is eating to maintain his normal growth and meet his body's energy requirements, and he instinctively knows how to do that.

Do you want your child to feel guilty because he hasn't eaten the meal you have worked so hard to purchase or prepare? No, of course not. There is going to be a long list of events in his life to feel guilty about. You don't need to add to it his natural lack of hunger late in the day. When he gets older he will learn that in certain social situations it may be polite to eat a little of everything to make the hostess feel appreciated. But you aren't the hostess—you are a parent who has fixed a meal to be offered to everyone, and they may or may not eat it.

Difficult as this may be, it is extremely important to avoid pushing your child to eat. If you fail to heed this advice, there are several unfortunate consequences that may occur. I list them below in hopes of further discouraging you from following this disastrous pathway.

UNHAPPY MEALS

We have only so many waking hours during the day, and if you work out of the home, your time with your child is even further limited. A large chunk of these precious moments comes at mealtimes. If as a parent you are pressurizing the mealtime subtly or overtly by trying to get your child to eat when he isn't hungry, you are turning what could be a relaxed time into a very unpleasant time for you and your child. You will be frustrated because your unrealistic expectation that your child should eat most, if not all, of his meal is not being met. Your child will be angry because he is being made to do something his body doesn't need to do. He may feel bad because he just can't meet your expectations, further damaging his self-esteem. If you have tried to make him feel guilty because he hasn't eaten any of his supper, you unfortunately may have succeeded.

If as parents you can't agree on whether you should be pushing the child to eat, this disagreement will permeate the atmosphere and make the meal an unhappy time. My parents seldom disagreed in my presence, but I can still remember the deep sadness that I felt when I heard them argue. I can only imagine how miserable some children must be when their mealtimes are filled with arguments about eating. An exchange such as: "Eat your squash or you are going right to bed!" "No, he doesn't have to eat his squash!" "Yes, he does. Listen to me, Ricky, your mother doesn't seem to care if you grow up to be big and strong. Eat your squash" is not the way to end the day.

The unhappiness that can surround a mealtime full of pressure can even affect what a child is eating. In 1969 scientists at the University of Minnesota did a study of mealtime behavior that showed children nine to eleven years old decreased their intake of vitamins A and C when there was criticism during the meal of activities not related to food. You can imagine that if the criticism was food-related, the decrease in eating may have been even more dramatic.

UNHAPPY RELATIONSHIPS

How you interact with your child about the issue of eating can be an early example of how you may relate over more-impor-

tant issues as the child gets older. If meals become power strug-
gles in which you are flexing your parental muscle, you are
establishing a relationship in which you are the master and the
child is the servant. While children need guidance and limit-
setting when it comes to safety, they thrive when they are
allowed to make their own decisions and live with the consequences on less critical issues.

I recently was reflecting on the style in which my parents
raised me. I had always felt that they had done a good job, but I
hadn't really analyzed what it was about their style that had
made them successful parents. It dawned on me that from an
early age they had allowed me to make many of my own decisions. Once I could ride a bicycle, I could go anywhere my little
legs could take me as long as I reported in at specified times. I
had to make some decisions for myself. Was catching minnows
and pollywogs while I was still in my school clothes a good
idea? Were there some consequences for a fluorescent-bulb-
smashing orgy that I and some other six-year-olds enjoyed?

When I reached adolescence I wasn't presented with a long
list of places that I shouldn't go or people that I shouldn't associate with. I was given a reasonable time to be in at night, and
nothing more was said unless I had gotten myself into some
kind of trouble, and then there would be appropriate consequences. Of course, my parents tried to create situations in
which I would be deciding between good and better choices.
Living in a small town meant that it was easier for them to have
a better sense of what I was up to than had we lived in a large
city. As I grew older and could wander farther from home, this
became more difficult. Nonetheless, the lessons that I learned
about making choices and assuming responsibility as I roamed
the neighborhood on my bike as a seven-year-old made the
more-difficult decisions about temptations such as alcohol and
drugs a bit easier to make. I looked on my parents as people

who trusted me and created an environment in which I could grow and learn. They were not ogres who made me do things just because they were the boss. Of course, they had the final say, and held a position of power and respect, but they didn't abuse the power or squander it on such minor issues as how many green beans I had to eat. I was limited in what I could snack on, but I was not told that I had to eat all my broccoli or I couldn't go outside to play after dinner.

If you adopt a parenting style that emphasizes your mastery over your child's eating behavior, you are setting a precedent that will have to be changed if you are to succeed in the long run. If you would like to end up with your grown children as your friends, then take a hard look at how you are parenting them now. Pick your battles carefully—green beans should not be one of them.

BACKLASH

If you coerce, bribe, and push your child to eat certain foods, you run the risk that he will rebel with behavior that will be exactly the opposite of what you intended. Some scientists have done experiments that demonstrated that when children were rewarded for drinking something, they initially consumed more of it, but when the reward was withdrawn, they ended up drinking less of it. If, however, the child was offered the new beverage without reward, their preference for it increased as the beverage became more familiar. It is almost as though the child becomes suspicious of your motives if you have to offer bribes to get them to eat something. They seem to be saying to themselves, "Why are my folks making this big deal. It must be a trick. As soon as the game is over, I'm stayin' away from this stuff."

EATING DISORDERS

While some physicians and psychologists doing research on the eating patterns of adolescents think that there may be some relationship with how food was presented when the child was young, there is currently no solid evidence to support a connection between eating disorders such as bulimia and anorexia and pushing young children to eat. However, I am sure you agree that by promoting a healthy attitude toward eating in your three-year-old daughter, you certainly aren't going to do her any harm as she reaches the challenges of adolescence. By allowing your young child to control her own food intake from a healthy menu free of parental coercion, you may be helping her learn important lessons of self-regulation and discipline at a time in her life when the stakes aren't quite as high as during adolescence. If you have already relinquished control of her appetite at age three, by the time she is thirteen, she will have had ten years of practice at making her own food decisions, and diet may be one less power struggle you will have to resolve. Anorexia and bulimia are frustrating and frightening conditions for both parents and physicians. If there is *any* suspicion that there is a relationship between pushing your child to eat and the development of eating disorders later in life, why take a chance?

STOMACHACHES AND VOMITING

It is not unusual for children to complain of stomachaches at dinnertime when they are faced with parental coercion or encouragement to eat when they aren't hungry or when they are presented with food that they really don't want to eat. Sometimes this pain is clearly a conscious invention in an attempt to avoid the pressure. In some cases, it seems as though the pain created by the tension is very real. The child usually complains of the pain during the meal, as they realize that they aren't going to be able to "clean their plate" or "finish their peas." In other more serious cases, the child will begin to complain of pain well before the meal starts so that they won't even have to sit at the table and endure any of the pressure. The ploy usually works rather well because it takes a hardened parent to force a child to eat who is suffering with a bellyache. However, some parents will try the "Those are probably just hunger pains" approach. Fortunately, this degree of misguided parenting is rare. Usually, the pain ends up forcing a trip to the pediatrician. Most of the time I can get things turned around by asking the child and parents about the nature and timing of the pain and doing a complete physical examination. If your child is having pain only at mealtimes, has regular bowel functions, is growing normally, and you are pressuring him to eat, the odds are overwhelming that the pain is related to the pressure and will stop when you back off and take an authoritative approach.

Several times each year I will encounter children for whom the parental pressure to eat is so great that they will actually vomit. Obviously, this phenomenon is quite impressive and can ruin the meal for the rest of the family. Often the trip to the bathroom to vomit precedes the meal, but I remember one three-year-old boy who would wait until he was seated at the table, and if he smelled a food that he knew he wasn't going to eat, he would vomit right on the spot. While his response may seem extreme, it was the only strategy that he knew would prevent his father from hounding him to finish everything on his plate. When I was able to convince both parents to swear a pact of silence about eating, the child's vomiting at the dinner table stopped in a week. I am surprised that some families are very slow to realize that the atmosphere at mealtime is the cause of the vomiting. Please don't let this happen to you.

There are scores of other less-dramatic behaviors in children who have been pressured to eat that I have observed over the years. These include hair-pulling, facial tics, and stuttering, to name just a few of the common ones. Headaches and tantrums are also near the top of the list. Either consciously or subconsciously your child may find that his misbehavior or complaints of illness will get him sent to the peace and quiet of his room, safely removed from the uncomfortable atmosphere of the dinner table.

While these symptoms of mealtime stress increase as a meal approaches, they are often evident all day long and may be triggered by other factors such as fatigue. I recall one four-year-old boy who began to stutter when his parents initiated a "clean plate" policy. His speech returned to normal when the rule was rescinded. However, the stuttering returned one month later when he prematurely gave up his nap. The point is that your child may respond with physical symptoms to a variety of tensions that can appear in his life. The pressure to eat when he doesn't have an appetite is just one of those stressors, but it is one that you can do something about. Most of the time picky eating is merely an annoying behavior that causes little more than parental concern. However, if you persist in pushing your child to eat, and continue to make it abundantly clear that he is not meeting your expectations, the psychological damage can be substantial. Chapter 14 will show you how to change your behavior and create a mealtime atmosphere free of tension.

DOES YOUR CHILD HAVE

A DRINKING PROBLEM?

Before you get too far into this book, we had better make sure that your child isn't a poor eater because he has a drinking problem. Most young children appear to eat poorly just because they are young children, and that's what young children do. In my experience the second leading cause of poor eating is excessive drinking. It used to amaze me how often some simple suggestions about limiting fluid intake would convert a picky eater to a child whose appetite no longer concerned his parents. When you think about it, the strategy makes perfect sense. If a two-year-old weighing 25 pounds chugs down a quart or a quart and a half of fluid each day (not unusual at all), could you at 125 pounds (5 x 25 = 125) drink five times as much fluid, or five to eight (5 x 1.5 = 7.5) quarts each day? Not likely! If you attempted the feat, you would certainly have no room in your stomach for solid foods and you would spend most of your day in the bathroom. In addition, the fluid is usually milk or juice, both of which are high in calories and would dampen any appetite. It is not uncommon for children who drink excessively to become malnourished because the beverages they consume are not nutritionally complete and displace foods with essential nutrients from their diet.

MILK BABIES

One of the most common forms of this problem can begin in infancy, but becomes very prominent in the second year of life under the common term of "milk babies." These children are usually kept on a bottle well after the first year of life, although the situation can occur in children who are breast-fed or even off the bottle. Because milk is deficient in iron, and because sometimes cow's milk can cause losses of blood (and hence iron) in the intestines, these children become iron deficient. This bleeding is usually microscopic and so the child's stools would appear normal to the naked eye. However, over months, the blood loss can be significant. Poor appetite is one of the major symptoms of iron deficiency anemia, and so these children have no incentive to eat and consequently are content to continue to drink and drink and drink to the exclusion of solid food. The anemia can gradually reach life-threatening proportions to the point that hospitalization and even a transfusion may be required. Fortunately, cases this severe are less common since the addition of iron to infant formulas. If the problem is detected early enough, merely restricting the child's milk intake and offering an iron supplement will be sufficient to turn the downward spiral around.

BEDTIME BOTTLES

So if your child is still on a bottle and is a poor eater, the first thing to do is to get him off the bottle. The most difficult bottles to remove are those that have become linked to bedtimes. Unfortunately, for most of these children the bottle has doubled as a pacifier and is necessary to help the child get to sleep. One of the first things to do is to begin to break that association. If the child is given a bottle at bedtime and naptime, you need to begin to create a separation in time and space between the bottle and the bedtime. For example, if you sit with the child in your lap in his room and give him a bottle and then place him in his bed, you could begin by moving your chair closer to the door by a foot or two each night. Eventually, you will have moved out in the hall and then into the living room. By this technique you are at least getting the bottle out of the bedroom.

When this geographic separation has been accomplished, you can begin to interpose other bedtime rituals between the bottle and putting the child in his bed. These could include lullabies, stories, prayers, to name just a few. As I said previously, I recommend Dr. Richard Ferber's classic, *Solve Your Child's Sleep Problems*. It may very well turn out that the solution to your child's poor eating is to bite the bullet and to begin helping him to develop good sleep habits. This is not as far-fetched as it sounds. I have seen scores of children who became better eaters after their parents and I confronted and solved their children's bedtime drinking problems.

If your child has evolved a pattern in which he "must" take a bottle to bed with him, you will need to resort to a little trickery. Of course, you could always take the bull by the horns and just plain throw the bottle away. This will not cause any permanent psychological damage, but it does mean that you must be prepared for up to a week of tough nights as he learns techniques for putting himself to sleep without a bottle. Another method is to gradually decrease the amount of milk (by about half an ounce every other night) until you are down to just a couple of ounces. Then gradually start to dilute this two ounces of milk with water (about one-quarter ounce every four to five days) until your child is going to bed with just two ounces of water. This small amount of plain water won't interfere with his appetite. What often happens is that the child will find that diluted milk doesn't taste very good and they just discard the bottle themselves. If the child still wants the two ounces of water, he can keep up that routine as sort of a wet pacifier until he is four or five years of age. Unlike milk and juice, water contains no sugar and so won't contribute to tooth decay. Although the nipple can deform the child's bite, this usually is not associated with permanent damage as long as the bottle is discarded by the time his second teeth are erupting. I would hope that it had been discarded *long* before this.

I have found that the weaning process works best if you actually write down the plan on your calendar or a piece of paper.

April 1	7 1/2 ounces
April 2	7 1/2 ounces
April 3	7 1/2 ounces
April 4	7 ounces
April 5	7 ounces
April 6	6 1/2 ounces
April 7	6 1/2 ounces

And so forth, then . . .

June 2	1 3/4 ounces milk, 1/4 ounce water
June 3	1 3/4 ounces milk, 1/4 ounce water
June 4	1 3/4 ounces milk, 1/4 ounce water
June 5	1 1/2 ounces milk, 1/2 ounce water

And so forth . . .

In this way the whole family is in on the plan. Whoever is fixing the next bottle need only refer to the schedule stuck on the refrigerator door. With the plan staring at you in black and white, you are much less likely to waffle and go back to your old erroneous ways. This kind of weaning can be very effective and relatively painless if you make the decreasing increments small enough. It can still be a tough haul, but stick to your guns. It is important for your child's health, his teeth, and his eating and sleeping habits.

BREAST-FEEDING

The unfortunate association between drinking and sleeping can be particularly frustrating if breast-feeding is the villain. I am a strong proponent of breast-feeding, but there comes a time in some children's lives when the negatives of nursing outweigh the positives. Usually, this involves sleep (the mother's sleep, that is) but, as with the bottle, it can become a nutritional problem as well. While mother's milk is the best food for an infant for the first six to nine months of life, the child's nutritional needs begin to outstrip what breast-feeding can offer. If your child is eating poorly and you are breast-feeding, then usually one of the answers is to stop breast-feeding. I would like to be able to suggest that you "cut back" breast-feeding, but I have found that most mother-child pairs have difficulty reaching a compromise on this issue. In most situations it seems to be an all or nothing phenomenon because in many cases nursing has taken on more than just a nutritional role. It is the child's pacifier for sleep, his comfort when he falls and bumps his head, and it is something that his mother enjoys doing and that gives her a sense of security as well.

What this often means is that when you have decided it is

time to wean, or the pediatrician is concerned about your child's growth and nutrition, that this process should be done without hesitation over a week at the longest. This may seem harsh, but it has been my experience that vacillation, starting and stopping the process, is far more trying on the child than a clear-cut decision on part of the parents that is carried out swiftly and honestly. If your child's eating is your major concern, and you are not troubled about getting up at night, then you can try merely cutting back the nursing to two or three specific times during the day. This will mean refusing the child when he asks to nurse unless it is at a predetermined "snack time." I will caution you that this is difficult to do, and I have not seen it succeed very often. This is one rare example of the advantage of bottle-feeding. Gradual weaning can be achieved more easily with a bottle. It also means that if your child still wakes at night to nurse that he will continue to do this unless you *completely stop nursing.* I understand that the weaning process can be very trying for mothers (and fathers), but if your child is eating poorly and taking multiple short nursings all day long, then putting an end to the nursing is the first (and sometimes only) step to take.

The same strategy that I suggested for bottles can be applied to breast-feeding. Begin by working your way out of the child's room and then interposing other rituals between nursing and placing him in the crib. Shorten nursings so that the child finishes them while he is still awake. This is a difficult process, but please do yourself and your child a favor and don't drag it out for months. A week or two is all that you should need. Call on all your resources for help. Talk to your friends who have been through it. Ask your husband to handle the wake-ups. Check with your pediatrician for reassurance that you are doing the right thing. Good luck, it is a struggle worth winning. The sooner the better. You can do it.

THE JUICE DECEPTION

In recent years it has become apparent to pediatricians and nutritionists that excess intake of juice has become an increasing health problem in some Western societies. There are many causes for this, but among them must be included the practice of selling juices, particularly apple juice, in ready-to-feed bottles. This presentation implies that it is something that children need. If the baby food companies are selling it, it must be part of the total nutrition package. *Wrong!* There is also the assumption that juice is good for you and has lots of vitamins. Well, at least it is better than a soft drink. *Wrong again.* Juice is better than soft drinks, but it is easy to get too much, particularly in a bottle, and it displaces important nutritious components of the child's diet. Scientists in this country have discovered that excess juice consumption is a definite cause of poor weight gain and growth. Too much juice often causes loose stools and may contribute to a condition known as toddler's diarrhea. One group of researchers has confirmed my personal observations that some children who overdrink juice will exhibit poor appetite, poor mealtime behavior, and poor weight gain, as well as diarrhea.

In my practice I discourage parents from offering juice in a bottle by suggesting that only formula belongs in a bottle. When a child is ready for a cup, he is probably ready for a little bit of juice. This can be as early as five or six months. By following this guideline the juice bottle never exists and so it never has to be removed. In addition, milk (as opposed to formula) bottles don't exist either. In an attempt to save money as the child gets older, parents will encourage cups of milk over bottles of formula. It may seem like a rather arbitrary guideline, but it will help make excess drinking less likely.

Another little rule for the first year of life that can make weaning easier is to never allow the child to hold his bottle all by himself. Around four or five months of age, children will begin to try to grab onto their bottle. This can be a proud moment for a parent, but if you relinquish your grip on the bottle to the child, the child will begin to think the bottle is his personal property. When it comes time for weaning, you are trying to take away something that the child has come to think of as his own. If, however, you have kept a tight grip on the bottle, you have made it clear that the bottle is yours and your child will leave it behind with you as he ventures out into the world by crawling and walking. This little trick makes weaning a more-natural process. By keeping the bottle firmly in your hands, it is more like a breast. These two gimmicks may be too late for you to use now, but if you have another child, you will be ready with a plan that works.

THE WANDER BOTTLE

Another major contributor to the problem of excess fluid intake is what I call the wander bottle. If your child is allowed to carry a bottle (be it milk or juice) around with him at will, this provides him unrestricted access to high-calorie fluids, which he is likely to take in large amounts. Sometimes this drinking is because he is thirsty, but often it appears to be just out of habit or as a way to pacify himself. These bottles should be thought of as lollipops or "all-day suckers" that can leave a sticky trail all over the house. You wouldn't think of letting your child wander around with a piece of candy all day. You should feel the same way about a wander bottle.

Of course, all of the fluid these bottles provide will diminish your child's appetite, but you should also consider the continuous contact of the sugared liquid with his teeth. It appears that this contact time is an important factor in the development of dental caries (cavities). For example, a bag of candy you consumed all at once at the beginning of the day should be less of a hazard than the same-size bag of which one candy was eaten every half hour over the course of the entire day. In the first case the healthier portion of your diet and the normal cleansing mechanisms in your mouth will have all day to work. On the other hand a candy every thirty minutes will leave sugar on your teeth almost all day long.

While we might be tempted to blame the manufacturers who make bottles out of plastic, which allows them to be carried around safely, we should really look to those of us who provide our children with them as the problem. Simply stated: *Do not allow your child to carry around a bottle!*

SURROGATE BOTTLES

I fear that many parents believe they have successfully weaned their child because he no longer has a bottle. However, too often the bottle has merely been replaced by one of the many bottle surrogates. These may appear in the form of sippee cups or any one of a variety of covered drinking devices with nonspill lids or integral straws. Simply replacing the nipple with some other sucking device does not change the potential for misuse. If the child is allowed to carry them around all day, they are still a wander container and can be criticized on the same grounds as the bottles. Unlimited access is still likely to result in a full belly and poor appetite at mealtime. Of course, we see plenty of adults wandering around with megacontainers of soda and other heavily sugared beverages and integral straws, but I am a pediatrician and count these people as lost souls beyond my assistance.

You may be wondering what you are supposed to do when

you are out shopping with your child and he gets thirsty. Dr. Wilkoff says no surrogate bottles, and there aren't any clean drinking fountains handy. I think that there are many situations in which a covered integral-straw drinking container can be useful. However, it should only contain water, unless it is a scheduled snack time, and it is something for the parent to carry tucked away out of sight.

THE VALUE OF WATER

There are several strategies you can employ when trying to solve your child's drinking problem. First, I must make it clear that we are not going to limit water intake. Only very rarely will healthy children overdrink water. One exception is the very young child in a swimming pool who may view the pool as his teacup and try to drink the whole thing. This is an unusual problem and generally is limited to children under eighteen months. Being aware as a parent can prevent it from occurring. The other exception is the child with such a strong sucking need that he will drain bottle after bottle of anything, even water, not because he is thirsty, but because he is obsessed with sucking. For this reason I would suggest limiting the amount of water given in a bottle (if you must give a bottle) to six ounces per day divided into three two-ounce servings. If this isn't enough to satisfy the child's sucking need, then he'll just have to adapt, which he will.

Trust in your child's natural thirst for water. In general, you should allow your child unlimited access to water in a glass or cup. Children (and adults) have widely varying thirsts and water plays a critical part in the maintenance of all our bodily functions. If you are going to limit high-energy drinks, you must allow the child to respond to his thirst. If the child refuses plain water, you know that he isn't really thirsty and is just look-ing for something sweet to drink. If your child's body is gen-uinely in need of fluid, he will accept water. I'll bet that you have been over estimating your child's fluid requirements. When you limit the juice and milk intake, it is likely that you will find that his total fluid intake will go down, and his solid food intake will probably go up.

You must learn to trust in your child's natural thirst and water's ability to quench it. Your child's internal drive for water is so strong that if he is not getting enough fluid, he will literally drink from the toilet. This grotesque situation sometimes occurs in children who have certain medical conditions such as undis-covered diabetes. I mention it not for its shock value, but only to reinforce the notion that your child's natural thirst doesn't care if it is juice, soda, or toilet bowl water. If his body needs a certain amount of water, it will get it, as long as he is physically capable of getting to the source. Obviously, for the infant who has yet to learn to crawl or walk, or who is confined to crib or playpen, this rule does not hold. Remember, however, this book is aimed at healthy children over the age of one, who by definition will be able to get around. I will remind you to think of thirst when your child is fussy. However, if you offer him water and he doesn't drink it, you can assume he isn't thirsty.

It is ironic that as we have become more civilized, and the safety of our water sources has improved over the last century or two, that the practice of drinking water as a beverage has fallen out of vogue. In one survey 72.5 percent of preschool children and 50 percent of infants never drank plain water. It is high time that we returned something as simple as water to its proper place in the diet of our children (and ourselves). I know that many of you are concerned about the safety of public water supplies. My friends in the field of water treatment tell me that most of these concerns are unfounded and are fueled by overly restrictive federal mandates that are sometimes political in origin. I feel perfectly comfortable drinking the tap water in our community. However, if you are worried and wish to spend money on "bottled water," I think that is fine. Just make sure that you offer it to your child. I would rather that he drink bottled water than high-energy drinks like juice and milk to excess.

In the last few years, several new juicelike beverages have appeared on the grocery shelves and—unfortunately—in the hands and mouths of young children. Sports drinks, flavored iced teas, and "fruit punches" with very little real fruit juice really have no place in the diet of young children. Your child's fluid requirements can be met safely and nutritiously with a combination of milk, 100 percent real fruit juice, and just plain water. The other beverages should be considered in the same category as candy—just something sweet to drink instead of eat. If your child is genuinely thirsty, there is no reason to give him anything other than water.

It should be unnecessary for me to say that soft drinks, soda, pop, or whatever you call it has no place in a small child's diet. This includes diet drinks, about which I have nothing good to say. If you have bought this book because your child is a poor eater and you are still giving your child soft drinks, you haven't really thought seriously about your child's nutrition yet. Remember, monkey-see, monkey-do. If you are drinking soda, it should be done when the child is in bed or away.

TAKE A SEAT

There are several solutions to the wander bottle problem. First, make the rule that if your child wants something to drink other than water, he must be sitting in his high chair or at the table. This little trick can often solve the problem because your child is now faced with deciding whether he wants to interrupt his play or TV show for a drink. Usually, he will decide it isn't worth it and will significantly decrease his excessive drinking and begin to eat better. This kind of limit-setting is a thoughtful way of achieving results. Without issuing an absolute "no," you are giving the child a chance to make a decision and often he will make the correct one. You aren't outright refusing him a drink, you are making it just a bit difficult.

REVERSE YOUR RULES

If you have restricted your child's drinking to table or high chair and you find that he still is not eating well, then you will need to revise your rules and create a limit for the amount of milk and juice he is allowed to drink each day. Remember, we are *not limiting water*. For a child under the age of two, this limit should consist of a four-ounce cup of milk with each meal and a four-ounce cup of juice with each of his two scheduled snacks. For the child over the age of two, these cup sizes should be increased to six ounces. You could broaden these limits to include a cup of juice with breakfast if the child ate well at breakfast.

Some of you who are near my age may be confused by the relatively small amounts of milk that I am suggesting. You probably remember Tinkerbell trying to get us to drink three eight-ounce glasses of milk each day while we were watching the *Mickey Mouse Club*, or one of the other Disney shows. Well, times have changed. We know that you can have too much of a good thing, and milk would be included as one of these things. In addition to its volume, which displaces food from your child's diet, there is concern about excess fat intake as well. I can predict that you are going to have trouble getting grandparents to accept this milk limitation, but stick to your guns—it's the right thing to do. You can always have them call your pediatrician if they don't believe me. She will probably tell them that after age two she recommends 1- or 2-percent-fat milk. Skim is usually not recommended because growing children still need some fat in their diet. The equivalent of one eight-ounce glass is probably a minimum that your child ought to consume each day. Don't panic if he occasionally slips below the amount that should be viewed as an average consumption over a week or two.

TOO MUCH OF A GOOD THING

If overdrinking is the most important correctable cause of picky eating, then snacking is a very close second. This always surprises me because I thought that "no, you can't have those——
—[crackers, cookies, chips, etc.] now because they will ruin your dinner" was part of every mother's standard admonitions. It certainly was one of my mother's. However, week after week I encounter children who eat 75 percent of their calories between meals and (of course) just pick at their food when it is time to sit down at the table.

I can recall a two-year-old who ate two cups of raisins, three cups of high-fiber cereal, a half cup of yogurt, and four peanut butter crackers each day, all washed down with an unlimited amount of apple juice. None of this eating was done at the table, nor did it occur on any semblance of a schedule. I wasn't surprised at his mother's complaint that he never seemed hungry at mealtimes. She was college-educated and felt that because she had never allowed her son to have traditional snack foods such as chips, cupcakes, and cookies that she had been doing the correct thing. Of course, she was only half right. She had done a good job at choosing nutritious snack foods, but her failure to set limits on their amount and timing had been her undoing. She hadn't realized that there can be too much of a good thing.

The parents whose child has a hearty appetite for a variety of foods at mealtimes can be quite flexible about snacks, unless, of course, the child is overweight. Because you are the parent of a picky eater, you must set limits on his between-meal eating to preserve his appetite for lunch and dinner. Here are some suggestions for gaining control over your child's snacking:

TWO IS ENOUGH

Even the most incorrigible picky eaters deserve two snacks per day, but only two snacks! If there are battles to be fought over food in your home, they should not be waged at mealtimes, when you are hoping to have a pleasant family sit-down. But confrontations over snacks are going to occur. These are the skirmishes that need to occur and be resolved in your favor.

It is very reasonable and nutritionally sound to draw the line at two snacks per day, one midmorning and one midafternoon. If your child complains that he is hungry at other times, you are perfectly justified in telling him that he can wait an hour or two until the next meal or snack. Continued whining and badgering should be met with consistent and appropriate discipline—for example, sending him to his room for a time-out. A critical component of coping with your picky eater is setting limits and two snacks per day is one of the most important.

Although the style of eating currently known as "grazing" has become popular in the last few years, it can easily degenerate into uncontrolled snacking, which isn't going to help your picky eater to develop better eating habits at mealtimes. One form of grazing that I see in the office and around town involves the use of sealable plastic storage containers. Many mothers keep a generous supply of dry cereal and fruit in their tote bags so that whenever their child is getting fussy or says that he is hungry, off pops the plastic lid and a handful or two of "healthy" snack food is distributed. This form of parent-assisted grazing is probably harmless for some children, but your picky eater will benefit by a firm two-snacks-per-day limit.

THE RIGHT TIME AND PLACE

To make it easier for you to limit snacks and to make the process somewhat more predictable for your child, set specific times and places for them. Don't be entirely arbitrary in your assignment of snack times. Listen to when your child usually tells you that he is hungry, but make sure the snack is not too close to the next regular meal. Obviously, the halfway point between two meals is a good place to start.

Because your child is too young to tell time, it helps to link the snack to some regular event, even in his life. For example, "Just after *Sesame Street*" or "Before we walk down to the mailbox" can help your child understand when to expect his next snack. This will help you both to keep his badgering and whining to a minimum. Your answer of "It's too early for your snack" is too open-ended and will only be met by the same inquiry ten minutes later. The answer "You know that when Mr. Rogers comes on you will have your snack" is much more likely to put an end to the whining. If it doesn't, "If you keep bugging me about the snack, you will have to go to your room" will!

Give your child's snack a place as well. By assigning a standard location to have the snack, you will further discourage grazing or "wander-eating." Take the time to sit down with your child. You can have a coffee break, and it will provide you with another opportunity to enjoy each other's company over some food. This is particularly important if mealtimes have become negative experiences. You don't necessarily have to pull a chair up to the table. You could choose to sit on the porch or outside on the lawn, but give the snack a special place as well as a beginning and an end. By making snacks a bit more important and distinct, you will take a giant step away from "snacking" as an unhealthy all-day activity and toward the concept of two snacks that are limited in their content and timing and therefore unlikely to adversely affect your picky eater's appetite at mealtimes.

CHOOSE HEALTHFUL FOODS

If you only offer your child nutritionally sound food for snacks, he will have no choice but to eat the right things. Salty foods such as chips, salted pretzels, and pickles can elevate your child's sodium intake to unhealthy levels. The taste for salty foods can easily escalate and may eventually contribute to the development of high blood pressure. Furthermore, the thirst created by salty snacks will make it more difficult for you to curb your child's drinking problem.

Snacks high in sugar and fat, such as some baked goods and most candy, are more likely to blunt your child's appetite than foods with a lower-energy content. Obviously, if your child is overweight (let your pediatrician help you define overweight), then you will want to be particularly careful to avoid these high-calorie snacks.

Fresh fruits and vegetables make the healthiest snacks because in addition to having only modest amounts of sugar and fat, they are often high in fiber and other minor nutritional elements such as vitamins and minerals that are often difficult to find in other foods. They are also less energy-dense, meaning that for the same volume of food ingested, your child will take in fewer calories and be more likely to be hungry when it comes to mealtimes.

While some children may enjoy fruit for snacking, it is usually more difficult to get them to accept vegetables, although it is always worth a try. Carrot sticks, celery stalks, and cucumber spears are among the more popular, but you must be careful about the choking potential of these vegetables, particularly for the child under two years of age. If your child balks at having only fruit and vegetables, I have found that a reasonable compromise can be achieved by offering one snack per day of something from the bread group, such as crackers, or even a cookie or two. Of course, it would be best to choose a cookie with a minimum of fat and sugar. A low-fat fig (or other fruit) bar would fit this description and offer a little fruit as well. However, it is important to hold the line at only one of these bread-group snacks per day. The other snack should be a fruit or vegetable. For example, if the child has two oatmeal cookies for his morning snack, then in the afternoon he could be offered a sliced apple or some cucumber spears. If in the morning he had eaten a half dozen mandarin orange slices, he could then have three or four whole wheat crackers for his midafternoon snack. Graham crackers in the morning and chocolate chip cookies in the afternoon would not represent a healthy offering. When possible, these snacks should be positive events, and your child should be allowed to choose from a wide variety of nutritional alternatives that he enjoys. But make it clear to him that only one snack per day will be from the bread group. Remember that just as with the timing of snacks, you must set limits. Battles fought here are likely to avoid wars at the dinner table.

A BANQUET ONCE A DAY . . .

EVERY DAY

The core strategy for coping with your picky eater really boils down to presenting him balanced and nutritionally complete meals in a pleasant atmosphere and then allowing his own natural instincts to take over. Now it is time to talk about creating that atmosphere. If your meals are becoming unpleasant events filled with tension and animosity, this trend must be reversed immediately. Not only does this emotional climate discourage your child from eating and may evoke complaints of bellyaches, it does little to strengthen the interpersonal bonds that hold your family together.

The creation of a pleasant atmosphere at mealtimes may do little toward getting your child to eat better. Picky eaters can be a stubborn lot. However, our real goal is to convert what has become a negative experience into one that the entire family can enjoy. If you can begin to see meals as events that you anticipate eagerly instead of ordeals to dread, you have taken a giant step toward successfully coping with your child's finicky appetite.

A CHANCE TO MAKE
MEALTIME QUALITY TIME

It should not surprise you that, in general, I think the American family is in pretty sad shape. Our staggering divorce rate is just one indication of the magnitude of the problem. The fact that in many households the TV is on all day long would lead me to believe that even if everybody is home, they aren't paying much attention to each other. With two working parents becoming the norm, the time a child can spend with either of his parents is limited as it has never been before.

The term "quality time" has crept into our language and its usage is growing at an alarming rate. For the most part the term is misused because it leaves the definition of quality to someone other than the child. Seldom is the child asked when he wants or needs the time. Usually, a parent approaches the child and says, "Now I have some time. What would you like to do?" By that time the child may just be tired and would probably be better off going to bed. At least we are beginning to acknowledge that our children need more time with us, but we still have a long way to go in achieving true quality time.

In the 1992 presidential campaign, the term "family values" became a hot topic. The fact that each political persuasion would like to claim this nebulous turf as their own is a clue that the nation at large feels bad about the state of the family and would like something done about it. Remembering that I am just a small-town pediatrician from Maine, I will tippy-toe around the political aspects of this issue. But if I can help you begin to feel better about how your own family is doing, then I have accomplished one of my professional goals. I think I can do it with a few simple suggestions.

If our hectic lifestyles are contributing to the decay of our families, what better place than mealtime to begin to restore a little sanity and a change of pace. Forget the concept of "quality," just plain time is hard enough to find. Unless you have won the lottery, work is a necessity and consumes a large portion of your day. Changing work schedules can be difficult. Though the concepts of "flextime" and job-sharing are beginning to catch on, the nine-to-five mentality seems to be etched into the landscape, at least for the near future.

The desire to flee the city means that commuting is going to gobble up some of your day. Suburban life can exact a steep price, costing many parents more than two hours each day in travel alone. Keeping your child involved in the great smorgasbord of extracurricular activities has its trade-offs. Soccer, gymnastics, piano, and dance lessons provide wonderful opportunities for your child. However, time in the minivan probably doesn't rank very high on the "quality" scale. There always seem to be trade-offs, and they never seem to generate more time.

But we all have to eat. You have already committed a certain portion of the day to this life-sustaining activity. Although your mother told you not to talk with your mouth full, dining remains one of those few activities during which it is polite to be doing two things at once: eating and socializing. With a little bit of extra effort, you can make at least one meal each day into a pleasant family gathering, free of the tension that fills the rest of our lives. The whole family may be happier and, lo and behold, your child may eat better in a pleasant, festive atmosphere. I must remind you that this increase in your child's appetite is not our goal here. Any improvement in your child's eating is merely a side effect, a bonus. The point is to convert what might have been a negative family experience into something positive. If we can create some good family time around a meal, we have come a long way.

Dinnertime, with a nice sit-down meal in the dining room,

was once the norm. As in most other cultures, dining was an integral part of family life in North America. In the introduction to her little treasure chest of "Things to Do at Dinner Besides Eating," titled *Whistling with Olives* (Ten Speed Press, 1996), my fellow Maine author Robin Hansen chronicles this unfortunate erosion of what could be one of our most positive family experiences. She concludes, "What we are facing today is the end of dinner as it has been celebrated among American families for centuries." While she may not be quite as optimistic as I am about our ability to restore dinnertime to its original place in our lives, she gives us a glimpse of how much fun a meal can be, even for the family with a picky eater.

FINDING THE TIME

For most families the evening meal is going to be the most logical choice for that together meal. Later in this chapter I will discuss how breakfast or lunch may be a more logical choice for other families, but for the bulk of this discussion, I am going to assume we are talking about the evening meal. Let's call it dinner (although I know some of you may refer to it as supper). The first order of business is to get a commitment from everyone in the family to be home in time for the meal. I realize that this can be difficult for many families, but compromises can be made. The decision to move attendance at dinner to a high priority may begin to set a whole new tone for family life in general. It may mean a new and more assertive you at the office. Can you hear yourself saying, "Mr. Strauss, do you think we could start our department meetings earlier? My family and I have decided that we all want to be able to sit down together for a meal once a day." It wouldn't hurt to ask, and he may be more sympathetic than you might think. Even if you can strike a bargain for a few days out of the week, it is better than nothing.

Sometimes your schedule compromise may mean that you come home for dinner and then return to the office to finish up or leave for a local school board meeting after you have all eaten. Of course, this may leave only one of you at home to participate in the bedtime ritual, but I think that this may be a very good trade-off. It is more important for your child to have a good early bedtime than it is to have you both present for the tuck-in. Likewise, if there is a choice between having you all there for dinner and bedtime, I would pick the meal.

I know some families that have set aside certain nights of each week as sacrosanct. For example, they might agree not to make any appointments Tuesday and Friday nights so that everyone can eat together. It is never easy to stick to these commitments, and as children become more involved in extracurricular activities, it can be downright impossible. However, if your children are still in preschool, defining a couple of special "at home" evenings each week may represent a workable compromise if you can't have a banquet every night.

All of this may mean that you are getting up earlier to get to work. You may have to move your aerobics to the morning so that you can work through lunch. Getting a good start early in the morning may have other benefits. You may be pleasantly surprised. Obviously, there are lots of ways to restructure family schedules. Be creative. I can remember one parent who agreed to work Saturday mornings so that he could get home early during the week. I have worked with families who have moved twenty miles closer to their workplaces primarily so that they could be home in time to have dinner with their children. Obviously, this is a major step, but these parents felt that they had exhausted all of their other options for creating family time out of thin air. I understand that making it home for dinner can be difficult and can't be achieved every night, but the result can certainly be worth the effort. Creating real "quality time" is not easy. It is going to take some work, but it will pay big dividends over the long haul.

WHEN DINNER JUST DOESN'T WORK

Not all of us (including myself) can always manage a work schedule that allows us to get home in time for an evening meal that is compatible with a child's sleep needs. Although at the beginning of the chapter, I admonished you to move this shared meal higher on the priority list, I understand that there are circumstances that are not easily avoided. If this is going to be a chronic problem, then there are several solutions. One is for the parent who is at home to have his or her meal with the children and try to salvage this as a family event. This parent might eat a full meal at this sitting and leave the late-arriving parent to eat alone after the children are down for the night. Another tactic is to have the parent eat a "snack" meal with the child, serving themselves such small portions that it won't interfere with a later meal. This can fool a young child, but obviously an older child will notice the difference. In this case the parent may just want to take the time and sit with the child to keep him company. This is certainly half a loaf and may not do much to encourage the child to eat, but we're emphasizing the positive social experience.

If your child's natural hunger peaks at five o'clock and there is no way that the rest of the family can be present or the meal ready by that time, you should feed the child his own meal early. To do otherwise would be cruel. However, you should set a place for him at the table for the second sitting when the rest of the family has assembled (assuming it is not after his bedtime). He can then pick and choose what, if anything, from your meal he would like to try. At a minimum he can share in the social experience. As he gets older and his hunger can hold off until you all get home, his early sitting can be abolished. Remember, my first choice would be for you adults to get home earlier, but I realize that even with extraordinary efforts, this isn't always realistic.

For some families the best solution is to make breakfast a major event instead of two Pop-Tarts on the run. This could be as extensive as the four-course old-style farm breakfast that we see in the movies and TV commercials. Or it could be as simple as getting the family to time their morning preparations so that everyone can sit down at the same time and not feel the need to rush off. Obviously, this means that people are going to have to get up earlier in the morning (and this usually means going to bed earlier at night). Bathroom activities will need to be streamlined, with extra need for sharing and compromise. That morning newspaper habit may have to be modified a bit. Hide in your office and read it at work. The result can be a pleasant gathering at breakfast, a meal your child is probably going to eat well anyway, which will help defuse some of your parental anxieties. You may find that even though you can do an evening meal together, you very much enjoy your two family meals—dinner *and* breakfast. Of course, breakfast may be a bit of a challenge if some of you aren't "morning people." I will acknowledge that some of us are better in the morning than others, but most of the time this can be explained by a bedtime that is too late, or a day that is overloaded in its latter half. Changes can be made. The cause is a good one. With some effort and compromise you can build a pleasant family event that includes eating.

Before our children reached school age, lunch became a good time for a family meal. We could usually do breakfast as well, but I often would get home too late in the evening for dinner.

However, my office is a five-minute bicycle ride from home, and so lunchtime was often our family time together. You might try a big midday meal on weekends.

THE FOOD

The title of this chapter should not be interpreted to mean that I expect each family meal to be a culinary epic. In fact, if time is a problem, I would urge that preparation be stripped to a minimum. Prepared or frozen meals, take-out, or food that is delivered to the home can still qualify for "banquet" status. It is the atmosphere and attitude at the meal that is most important. The content can fluctuate in culinary quality without jeopardizing the basic concept of a positive family experience. A take-out pizza and a salad can be almost as special as Thanksgiving if the atmosphere is just right. I am not suggesting that you compromise the nutritional value of your meals. The variety and distribution of nutritional elements should follow the guidelines in chapter 18. Remember that we are talking small children here who probably aren't going to appreciate the time you have spent in preparation. In fact, it is likely that your picky eater isn't going to eat much of anything, so don't feel pressed to create culinary excellence. If you and your spouse want a special gourmet meal, hire a sitter and go out on Saturday night. If you do have the time and want to cook fancy at home, do it, but don't be offended by the underwhelming response from your picky eater.

SETTING THE SCENE

If your home has a dining room, obviously that is a place for the banquet. If you are not fortunate enough to have a separate room for eating, do what you can to create a space that is a little special. Flowers or a centerpiece of some sort can provide a visual focal point that can help you forget you are sitting at a table in the kitchen. The children can even participate in picking out something that they would like for the centerpiece. A tablecloth can be a nuisance to wash, but it can add a festive touch to an otherwise ordinary room and meal. Cloth napkins and napkin rings are even more elegant and can provide materials with which to play games as the meal winds down.

The process of getting out the tablecloth and putting it on can serve as a signal that a meal somewhat more special than breakfast and lunch is about to begin. Folding screens and drapes can create a sense of separation from the clutter and distractions of the rest of the house. Do whatever you can do to create a place of relative tranquillity. This includes unplugging the phone. Put it on the answering machine and turn down the volume of the ring. We are only talking twenty minutes here. Whoever it was can wait until you are done.

TURN OFF THE TV!

Television probably creates the single biggest distraction when it comes to mealtime in the American home. In fact, in one survey published in 1991, television was on during mealtime in 54.5 percent of the families. In 16 percent of the households, the TV was on all day long. Sometimes no one has thought to turn it off and it is still blaring away in the adjacent room. In other homes everyone has opened up their TV tables and is eating in the living room, and in other situations the TV is in the dining area just as if a noisy guest pulled up to the table. If we are going to make this one meal an event that is going to emphasize interaction among the family members, let's remove the number-one distraction.

Turn off the TV. If there is something you really want to watch, use the VCR to tape it and show it when the meal is over. Those electronic gadgets aren't that hard to program. Let's not be slaves to technology, but let's have it work for us and improve the quality of our life. Certainly, if there is something "live" that is of momentous interest, there can always be exceptions. Lunar landings or Super Bowl games are two examples of times when it might make sense to subordinate the family meal to what is on the tube. However, most news events aren't really "live," and so lose little if delayed half an hour to accommodate a nice family meal.

I think many pediatricians would agree with me that the problem with TV is not so much what shows are on, but that it is on too much. Viewing TV is basically a passive endeavor. Your child can do very well with just one hour of TV each day. Let's get them living life and not spending their whole time on the sidelines watching someone else's life or idea of what life should be. You should have a good handle on your child's TV viewing and a great place to start is leaving it off during mealtimes.

CREATING THE ATMOSPHERE

With the TV off and some minimal effort to dress up the table, you have gone a very long way to making your evening meal a little special. There are a few more little things you can do to make the atmosphere more conducive to a pleasant family dining experience. First, you can turn the lights down and put a candle on the table. It's an old trick that cheap and expensive restaurants alike have been using since the invention of the electric light. Think about investing a few dollars in a dimmer switch for the overhead light. They aren't that difficult to install; I have done it myself several times. Unless it is late June or early July and sun is still blazing in at dinnertime, we *always* have a candle on the table, even if we have ordered pizza. With the lights a little dimmed and a candle on the table, the hectic pace of the day seems to slow, and even the most rambunctious child will be unwound a notch or two. I will stop short of suggesting soft music on the stereo (we aren't talking romance here) and I can foresee arguments about what exactly constitutes appropriate music, but it is hard to quarrel with the effect of candlelight. In our family, even after more than twenty-five years, the candlelight creates an atmosphere that we all enjoy.

FIRST, A PAUSE

We have also found that beginning dinner with a pause can further emphasize that the next twenty minutes are going to be a special time set aside from the helter-skelter of the rest of our lives. This pause can be in the form of a prayer or blessing or it can be a toast. Sometimes just beginning the meal with a word of thanks to the cook can serve the same purpose. In our family we bounce back and forth between blessings and toasts depending on the day and who is at the table, but we always have some pause that both relaxes us and gets us into a more positive frame of mind. This pause is a signal that a special family event, our evening meal, has begun. It will be a time to enjoy each other's company and hear how we're all doing. In the process we will have something to eat, but foremost we are going to enjoy ourselves.

IT'S A BANQUET, NOT A ROAST

The candlelight, the tablecloth, the pause at the beginning of the meal, can all help to create a pleasant ambience, but all of this can be for naught if someone comes to the table with an ax to grind. I realize that none of us are members of the Brady Bunch, and that there are serious issues that weave their way through the fabric of every family. I am not advocating that these conflicts be ignored, but there is something to be said for trying to keep the evening meal as free from turmoil as possible. There are much better times to confront the issues that often crop up even in the most well-adjusted families.

As parents you can set the example for appropriate behavior at the dinner table. Try first to share the positive aspects of your day. "Brad, what do you think I saw nibbling on Mrs. Murphy's flowers as I left for work this morning?" "Louise, I told Mrs. Stevens about that painting you did at day care yesterday, and she wants me to bring it to work tomorrow so she can see it. I hope you didn't throw it away." These are examples of statements that describe part of your life, but involve the child in the conversation.

The meal can also be a time to describe some of the frustration that you have encountered, but the rest of the family will tire if this is your only tune. Night after night and meal after meal, complaints can become monotonous and certainly are not conducive to a pleasant social gathering. If you told them Monday night that your boss is an idiot, they don't really need to hear it at dinner on Tuesday, Wednesday, and Thursday as well, unless you can support your complaint with a humorous anecdote. The old homily "If you can't say anything nice, don't say anything at all" is probably a bit of an overstatement and could result in total silence some evenings. A more workable and effective rephrasing of the adage might be "If you don't have anything positive to say, ask someone else how their day went before you complain about yours." It is a good practice to go around the table and ask each family member what in their day they wanted to share. This should not be in the form of an inquisition or a command performance. The shy child may not be comfortable speaking "publicly" even in the relative warmth of his family. In other words offer everyone at the table a chance to contribute, but by no means demand a speech. You are trying to create a relaxed atmosphere for everyone, and you need to be sensitive to the comfort levels of each family member.

Think how uncomfortable you have felt when you were invited for dinner and ended up hearing the other couple carping at each other all night. Maybe you were unfortunate enough to have a father who would use the dinner table as his own personal soapbox to rage at the injustices of the world. I'm sure that neither situation did very much for your appetite. Keep these unpleasant experiences in mind when it's your turn to speak.

You must also reaffirm your sworn oath that neither your child's picky eating nor a restatement of the family's eating rules is a topic for discussion during the meal. The child already knows you don't like it when he doesn't eat his lima beans. He knows that he won't get seconds on the macaroni until he has finished his peas. There is no need to remind him again during the meal. There is no place for the statement "You know that if you want to make it as a football player that you better finish your meal." This doesn't mean that food cannot be discussed— it is a most natural topic—but as we have observed in chapter 11, picking on the picky eater is going to be counterproductive and should *not* be done!

FUN AND GAMES

Dinnertime isn't all about eating—in fact, for your picky eater, it may not be about eating at all. This doesn't mean that your child can't enjoy himself at the dinner table. We want to convert your family meal from an event dominated by tension and conflict to a harmonious gathering at which a good time is had by all. To do this you can inject some fun and games that even your picky eater can enjoy. I am not talking about little contests such as "How many peas can you eat?" or "Let's see how many lima beans you can get in your mouth." I am talking about the scores of little stunts and near-magic tricks that have been passed down at dinner tables in this country for generations, none with any hints of coercion to get your picky eater to finish his peas.

Activities like making music by running a moistened finger around the rim of a drinking glass, or hanging a spoon on your nose, can enliven what might have been a disappointing meal for a child who wasn't hungry for anything he was offered. For the older child games such as Twenty Questions or "I'm thinking of something . . ." can replace the more physical comedy of making fingers, thumbs, and noses disappear.

As those at the table who are eating have begun to finish up, you can entertain requests for some postmeal activities. Take advantage of this time together, free of the TV din. Have some fun with each other, elbow to elbow, face to face. An extra ten or fifteen minutes of time at the dinner table can help your child see mealtimes as a fun time, not a time of repeated failure. Instead of just one more night when he isn't going to clean his plate, it will be another chance to see if he can guess under which teacup you have hidden the lima bean, another chance to play with Mom and Dad. Remember the good times you had as a child at Thanksgiving when Uncle Elliot would play some rhythms on the spoons? Why wait for Thanksgiving? Just as you are going to start each meal with a pause to set the tone, you can finish every meal with a little family entertainment and amusement to remind yourselves that you are a family that can have fun together.

JUST DO IT!

You may feel that some of the suggestions in this chapter won't work for your family. The "every night" part of it just seems unachievable. The candlelight sounds hokey. That's okay—these are just suggestions. It's more important that you see my basic premise as something you want to try. If I have nudged you into wanting to make more of your meals into events that foster a sense of family, then I have succeeded. Even if it is one or two nights a week, that is far better than not at all. If you all think that subdued lighting and tablecloths are too formal, and that makes you uncomfortable, then develop your own setting. The point is that with "together time" in such short supply that we have to label some of it as "quality," make mealtimes into something special. Create an environment in which meals will be events your child will look back on fondly. It's really not that difficult. . . . Just do it!

JUST DESSERTS

(OR NEVER SAY NEVER)

Is there a place for desserts in the diet of a picky eater, or any other child for that matter? I have told you that it is counter-productive to bribe your child by offering him a dessert as a reward for eating his peas. I have also told you that when your child eats high-energy, or high-calorie, foods, they tend to displace more nutritional foods from his diet. It sounds as though a responsible parent should go right ahead and abolish desserts from the house menu and be done with it. You can try this and there may be households where a no-dessert policy succeeds, but I think you are looking for trouble. The rest of the world, with its rack after rack of cookies and snack cakes, is not going to go away. Your child lives under your watchful eye for a very few years. After that he will venture out into the world of junk food and many more serious temptations. If you believe that by forbidding desserts in your house you are going to protect him from these less-nutritious foods, you have your head plunged pretty deep in the sand.

FORBIDDEN FRUIT

You must realize that children, like most of us, tend to be attracted to things that we have been warned against, but in which we see no obvious danger. The magnetism of the forbidden is terribly strong, and this is particularly true if we have had an opportunity to taste of the forbidden fruit. It seems that the more you enforce a taboo, the more your child wants to experience the pleasure that you are withholding. Sometimes it's just a power struggle to be won for the sake of winning, and the object can become lost in the battle. You may begin to wonder if it is worth the fight.

FINDING A COMPROMISE

When our son was young, he wanted a toy gun. My wife and I had decided that we weren't going to support the violent use of guns by purchasing even a toy one for him. He protested a little, but seemed to let it drop after a few weeks. He did, however, have a toy chainsaw (a logical toy for a child here in Maine), which he began to use as a toy weapon, threatening to dismember his opponents. We realized that guns weren't going to go away and neither was a young boy's natural tendency toward mock violence. We lifted our ban on guns, and he and I spent an afternoon making a toy gun out of wood, talking about gun safety and the difference between real violence and play. In relaxing our restriction we had replaced an unenforceable rule with something that made sense to our son and offered the opportunity for learning some important concepts.

This incident was also a good example of how involving your child in a process, particularly if there is a hands-on component, can result in a solution that he will accept because he has something invested. For the picky eater this translates into participating in the planning and preparation of a meal. Ask your child what foods he might like. Help him select one that is nutritionally sound, and enlist his assistance in preparing it. While this process may be time-consuming, it is time spent together and will help him view food in a more positive way.

DEFINING DESSERTS

How can you apply the strategy of my son's toy gun to the dessert dilemma? On the one hand you know that desserts aren't really good for your child, but on the other, if you absolutely forbid them, you are inviting endless conflict and run the risk that your efforts will backfire and desserts will be more attractive to him.

First, let's define desserts. I really should have used the word "sweets" to distinguish them from fruits. If you are going to offer fruit as part of the meal, it should be presented *with* the meal and not held out as a reward. Fruit could conceivably be offered with every meal and not destroy the balance of nutrition. Sweets, on the other hand, include such things as ice cream, frozen yogurt, cookies, and cakes. If they were offered at each meal, it is likely that the child, particularly the picky eater, would choose them in preference to the more nutritious food. How, then, should desserts be offered, if you are going to offer them at all?

UNCONDITIONAL DESSERTS

The answer begins with an understanding between you and your child that we all deserve a special treat every now and then. Desserts may not be particularly good for us compared with the rest of our diet, but as long as we eat them in moderation, they aren't going to ruin our lives. By taking this attitude you are defusing some of the explosive potential that can develop by making sweets forbidden. Your child will begin to see you as a more-compassionate parent, someone who has some flexibility, someone who knows how to have a good time now and then, and someone who knows how to set limits that make some sense.

So now we have agreed that you are going to offer desserts, but remember they should be *unconditional desserts*. In other words your child is going to receive his sweet at the end of his meal just like everyone else, even if he didn't clean his plate, even if he didn't finish his peas. Remember that bribery and coercion have no place in the management of a picky eater. Conditional desserts are counterproductive in that they won't get the child to eat better in the long run and they tend to focus more attention on the sweet.

PRESENTING DESSERTS

Desserts should be offered just because it is time to treat yourselves to something special. There are many ways to do this. It could just be spontaneous and unannounced. If you notice that the child has eaten particularly well, you might "silently" reward that behavior with a dessert. This means you do not mention nor allow the inference that you are offering dessert tonight because the child has eaten well, you just do it. If you need to say something, you might say, "It's been a long time since we had dessert. Why don't we all have a little bowl of ice cream?" Or "We've all had a nice day, why don't we celebrate and have some cookies?" You might regard this approach as somewhat sneaky, but if properly done, it may help encourage your child to eat better—without the downside of outright bribery.

Another system for offering desserts relies on a schedule. For example, you can develop a family tradition that every Friday night is dessert night, even if the child hasn't cleaned his plate. In adhering to a predetermined schedule, you will guarantee that desserts are unconditional. I am assuming that you will be prudent in your choice of portion size for the Friday-night specials. Two cookies, a one-inch wedge of cake (or one cupcake), or two golf-ball-sized scoops of ice cream are examples of what I mean by prudent.

Two dessert nights each week would seem to be sufficient and not excessive. You and your family may view this limit as overly restrictive. If your child is a good eater and no one in the family is overweight, you could have more frequent desserts. However, your child's picky eating may create an opportunity to look at your own eating habits. Limiting yourself and the rest of the family to two desserts per week will probably be good for everyone in the house. The schedule does not preclude the occasional spontaneous dessert; in fact, the addition of an impromptu treat can serve to de-emphasize the whole process.

Desserts should be served at the same sitting as the meal; otherwise, they ought to be considered a very bad choice for a snack. They should not be delayed because people are "too full." In fact, having them right after the meal might help encourage keeping the serving size to a reasonable amount. Converting the dessert to a bedtime snack is not a good idea because this can set up a bad pattern for the future, when your picky eater may have a problem with excess weight. Calories consumed late in the day are more likely to stick on your body as fat than those ingested earlier, when exercise will tend to burn them off.

Desserts present a tangible and eatable example to your child of your flexibility and humanity. Yes, you are a parent who sets reasonable limits that you enforce firmly, but you also know how to have a good time at the dinner table and sometimes that means a dessert, even if everyone didn't clean their plates. The proper attitude toward sweets can enhance your image with your child and at the same time show him that even some naughtiness can creep into a healthy diet and be kept in sensible balance.

HOLIDAY DESSERTS

Special occasions are often a time for desserts and treats. Christmas, Hanukkah, Halloween, Easter, and Thanksgiving are obviously intertwined with food traditions that include sweets. Even the picky eater deserves some of the traditional high-energy foods from these holidays. They, too, should be unconditional but kept in moderation. This advice applies not just to the picky eater but to everyone in the household. These festive events are a good time to emphasize the social aspects of a meal. I hope that you have been employing some of the strategies you read in chapter 14 and make at least one meal a day a banquet, but these special holidays can become real banquets in which religious and family traditions can be woven around the process of eating. Even the finicky eater can sense the excitement that these festivities can generate, although he may not be a full participant.

When the holiday is over, you could have difficulty getting your picky eater back on track. He may have trouble accepting "No seconds unless you have cleaned your plate," on the Monday after Thanksgiving, when he has been able to eat his fill of black olives and pumpkin pie without even the slightest comment by anyone about his failure to eat his squash or broccoli. There is no easy answer to helping him shift gears back to business as usual, except to make it clear that there is a distinction between holiday behavior and the real world. It may take him a few days to make the transition, but your usual rules and limits should be applied as soon as the holiday is over. Of course, you should make it clear before the holiday that this transition will occur and exactly when it will occur. A firm and matter-of-fact approach on your part will help him realize that the party is over.

SO NOW WHAT DO YOU OFFER?

Our knowledge of the nutritional requirements for a growing human body is surprisingly scanty considering that we have the scientific skills to put a man on the moon. Just think of all the flip-flops we have witnessed in the last few years on such things as cholesterol, eggs, and oat bran. Many of the experiments of the so-called nutritional experts use animals and may not apply to us. The human studies have often involved accidental or intentional causes of starvation. Sure, we know what happens if a sailor is shipwrecked on a desert island and doesn't have any fruit or vegetables—he eventually develops scurvy—but that doesn't really tell us how much vitamin C the average five-year-old needs every day. Scientists discovered that if you gave baby mice a diet that was deficient in fat, their brain and nervous system failed to develop normally. However, this experiment doesn't tell us exactly how many grams of fat your three-year-old daughter should be eating.

FINDING CORRECT ANSWERS

No one really has all the correct answers about what food to offer your picky eater. The experiments of nature and in the laboratory have often been at the extremes of nutritional requirements, and may not apply to our everyday diets. We know quite a bit about what happens if you eliminate certain elements of the diet, but we have very little understanding of the optimal amounts of these substances to put on the table.

Ignorance and controversy abound in the field of nutrition. Wherever there is a vacuum, fad and quackery will fill in. It is difficult for people to accept that traditional science doesn't have many of the facts when it comes to nutrition. Bookstores have shelf after shelf of books claiming to have the solution to this or that problem through special diet. Although year after year the American Dietetic Association tells us that vitamin supplements are unnecessary for the average American, we continue to buy them by the billions.

We all keep hoping that there is a book out there somewhere that has the answers, but there isn't. In reality, the solid truth about nutrition could be contained in a six-page pamphlet, and some would even say on a three-by-five card. Most of us don't even realize that the RDA (recommended daily allowance) is a concept that was developed to assist in planning food supplies for public programs and populations. Those numbers that you find covering the sides of cereal boxes have no bearing on real life.

I wish I could remember the name of the professor in school who told me that good nutritional advice could be summed up in the phrase "Everything in moderation." That was thirty years ago and I think the statement still holds up. Just think about the revelations and rerevelations we have had in the last few years about things as basic as eggs and oat bran. The flip-flops on these topics should make you very skeptical about pronouncements by anyone claiming to be an expert on nutrition.

Fear not, despite these reservations about the wisdom written in both traditional and nontraditional nutritional texts, I am going to lay out some simple guidelines for creating a healthy, balanced diet for your child. If I didn't think salt was such a bad thing, I would tell you to take them with a grain of it.

HOW MUCH?

Remember, I am going to suggest approximately how much food you should *offer*. By definition, your picky eater is not going to eat everything you have put on his plate. So, please, *please,* do not think that these suggested amounts indicate what your child should *ingest* at each meal. They are only general guidelines to help you decide how much to *serve* and often represent more than the child needs. If you finish this chapter feeling that you now have a list of what your child should eat every day, then I have failed. Instead, your comfort should come from knowing that you have learned how to create a balanced and healthy diet that even a picky eater can thrive on.

YOUR MENUS AS A COMPROMISE

If figuring out how much to offer is more art than science, then planning what to serve is pretty much all art. As you will read in chapter 17, there really are only four basic food groups to consider. However, mixing and matching these groups into a menu that will keep your family happy requires imagination and an aptitude for crafting compromises. Even in the best of circumstances choosing foods that will please everyone at every meal can be difficult, if not impossible. But if you have a picky eater in your family, you are guaranteed to fail. Unless, of course, you ignore my advice and prepare every family member his or her own selection at each meal.

The solution is to view your family menu as a compromise. For example, tonight we will have a main course that is on your preferred list and the vegetables will be on mine. Tomorrow the main course will be my favorite and the vegetables will be yours. You probably were already doing this unconsciously with your spouse before you even began to think about having children. However, if one of you always feels that he or she is getting short-changed when it comes to menu selection, it is time for you both to sit down together and have a little discussion before we can go any farther. It probably means that we have *two* picky eaters in the family and that one of them is a parent. It is going to be very unlikely that your child will "outgrow" his picky eating if one of his primary role models still exhibits this kind of behavior. I would urge you now to look into yourselves to see where you can change your eating behaviors. If nothing else, parenting is about setting a good example. "Actions speak louder than words." "Do as I say, not as I do." They are old saws, but they do convey an important message.

If one of our goals is to have pleasant family meals, then some of them should include foods from your picky eater's limited list of favorites. Of course, the meal still must meet the minimum standard of having all four food groups, which is usually not that difficult to achieve. Obviously, this means that your weekly menu is going to have a more childish character than it did before your child was born, but life is about compromise. Child-rearing is about compromise. If you want to have pleasant family meals, then your menu must be a compromise, but a healthy compromise.

For example, it is likely that you may have spaghetti twice a week because your child will eat it, although when left to your own choice, once every week would be just fine. You can always let people have a choice of two simple sauces for variety. Corn is often a vegetable that young children will tolerate. It might be nice for the whole family to have corn twice each week, though three times a week is a bit of a stretch. Is that too much to ask? I don't think so.

If there are certain expensive foods that you are craving, and you don't feel like wasting them on your picky eater, then there can be an occasional night (not more than once a week) when you *and* the child get their favorites. For example, you and your spouse share some swordfish, and the picky eater gets chicken nuggets or a can of low-salt spaghetti. As long as the inconvenience in preparation is minimal and the "everyone's-favorite-night" doesn't become a daily occurrence, I think it can fit nicely into the pattern of compromise I am suggesting. Remember, *everything in moderation,* and that includes moderation. There is a difference between flexibility and letting the child call all the shots.

THE ART OF PRESENTATION

Choosing the quantity of each component of the meal to place on the plate is really more of an art than the result of precise measurements and calculations. How the food appears to your child may affect his willingness to venture beyond his very few favorites. You might ask, "Why not just serve an excess of each item and then let the child eat his fill?" While it might work in the very long run, that philosophy has a few problems. First, the child may eat so much of his favorite food that he won't have any hunger incentive left to try the things that he traditionally shuns.

Remember the rules from chapter 9. No seconds until everything in the first offering has been finished. For example, if the meal is macaroni and cheese and peas and you have served too large a portion of macaroni, the child will be satiated before he even gets to his peas. Hence, your decision about serving size for your child's favorites must take into account your past observations of how much of them your child can and will eat. By erring *slightly* on the small side, you will create the opportunity for some hunger-induced adventuring. However, don't overdo on this downsizing. We are not trying to starve your picky eater, we just don't want him to eat to excess.

When it comes to the shunned foods, you also want to be careful not to overdo with quantity. One consideration may be waste. There is no sense in throwing away good food, but more relevant is the "Everest factor." Look at the plate through the eyes of your picky eater. If you have presented him with a mountain of lima beans, there is no hope that he will ever get to the bottom of them. He will never get to have seconds on macaroni and cheese. The prospect of that huge mound of something he doesn't like is not helping him to have a pleasant mealtime. He is not going to tackle it just "because it's there." Serve him just a little pile of beans, a token, an amount that he has some hope of finishing. For a two-year-old this could be a tablespoon, for a five-year-old two tablespoons. Give him less than you think he should eat; he is probably not going to eat it anyway.

These amounts are just starting points. If and when he gets to the point of finishing his shunned foods (it could be a decade later), then you can slowly increase the size of the mound. Although you have promised to keep mum about his eating pattern, your child knows how you feel. He really does want to please you. Give him a chance to succeed.

For all of these reasons I want you to view the suggested quantities of food as very rough approximations, ballpark figures at best. They are to be tempered with good sense and presented artfully, keeping the issues I have just cited in mind. I am not a numbers kind of guy, and I don't want you to be weighing and measuring portions in sight of your child. If you really must do it in the beginning, do it on the sly.

Before we get to the recommended offerings, there are a few special issues that I need to discuss with you. For the most part these are topics that have either received considerable media attention or about which there is more myth than truth. If you are going to present a healthy, balanced meal to your picky eater, you must have a good understanding of these nutritional elements.

WHAT'S THE PROBLEM WITH SUGAR?

I think that most parents in North America would agree that sugar is something that should be avoided in a healthy diet. When asked why, they would probably include hyperactivity as one of their reasons. Unfortunately, the notion that sugar contributes to hyperactivity cannot be supported by solid scientific research. In 1995 a group of pediatricians at Vanderbilt University reviewed all the relevant research about sugar and behavior. They subjected the studies to rigorous data analysis and found that in summary sugar had not been proven to contribute to hyperactivity.

Why, then, do so many people think that their children are "wired" by sugar? My own guess is that many of the situations in which children get excesses of sugar are also occasions when they are sleep-deprived or overstimulated. For example, the holidays of Christmas, Easter, and Halloween are certainly candy-oriented, but they are also times of great excitement and physical and emotional exhaustion. Anyone familiar with small children is aware that many of them become more active as they become fatigued. As far as I know, no one has a scientific explanation for this paradoxical hyperactivity, but it certainly does occur. There is some evidence that a very small percentage of children who have been diagnosed with ADHD (attention deficit and hyperactivity disorder) are made worse by some artificial dyes and food colorings. However, most children with ADHD are not made worse either by food colorings or sugar. So it looks as if we won't be able to blame sugar for our children's bad behavior.

However, there are some legitimate reasons to keep the sugar content of your child's diet to a minimum. One of these is dental caries. While it has become apparent that inheritance and bacterial infection are major causes of cavities, the sugar content of a child's diet is also a contributor. The contact time also seems to be a factor. In other words, if you had a lollipop that took you a half hour to finish, it would be worse than if you had pulled it off the stick and swallowed it whole. This is the same principle behind one of the arguments against wander juice bottles. If teeth are bathed in a sugar containing solution all day long, they are more likely to develop cavities.

Probably the most important reason to keep the sugar content down in your child's diet, particularly for a picky eater, is that sugar provides what one might call "hollow" calories. What I mean is that sugar does not provide the kind of raw material for building and repairing young bodies that protein provides. When compared with the other more complex carbohydrates, foods high in sugar do not contribute other essential nutrients, such as vitamins, minerals, and fiber. In simplest terms, if your child fills up on high-energy foods, such as those with a high sugar and/or fat content, then he won't be hungry for the foods that are better for him. Fresh fruit, however, is an example of a family of foods that may be high in sugar, but also contains other nutritional elements, including vitamins and fiber.

Let's also remember that sugar is sugar. Whether it is cane, beet, refined or unrefined, brown or white, sugar is still sugar. Dumping a huge scoop of brown sugar on your child's breakfast cereal should make you feel no better than an equivalent amount of pure white granular sugar.

Parents and scientists agree that almost all children have a natural preference, present at birth, for sweet things. It certainly makes sense that even the nonpicky eater will eat the sweet things first. However, do not take this as an admonition to avoid all sweet foods in your family's diet. There is nothing wrong with jam on whole wheat toast as part of breakfast, or fruit-flavored yogurt as an occasional milk equivalent.

CHOLESTEROL

Few nutritional elements have received more public attention in the last ten years than cholesterol. We read about it daily in the newspaper, see documentaries on TV, and talk about it among ourselves at cocktail parties and picnics. While scientists have agreed that an elevated cholesterol plays a role in the development of heart disease, it has only recently been shown that lowering cholesterol can actually reduce a person's risk of heart attack. Prior to that research, physicians were recommending prudent diets and occasionally prescribing medication because it seemed likely to help, but they were unsure if these steps would really make a difference in the long run.

When it comes to children there is still considerable uncertainty about what to do about cholesterol. We do know that a large number of cholesterol problems are inherited, and that children in families with early heart attacks and stroke victims already have elevated blood cholesterol while they are young. However, we are not completely sure what to suggest to the parents of these children. Since cholesterol and other lipids are important for normal growth and development, an overly restrictive diet and/or medication might be dangerous.

As of the writing of this book, the American Academy of Pediatrics recommends that if your or your spouse's family history includes people with early heart attacks or stroke (before the age of fifty-five) or who have cholesterols of 240 or greater, then your child should be tested at about two years of age. Universal testing is not recommended. For example, a blood cholesterol test is not being suggested for all five-year-olds entering kindergarten.

If your child is tested and has an elevated cholesterol, then you and your pediatrician will sit down and discuss the treatment options. Usually, someone else in the family is already on a low-cholesterol diet, and this will be extended to include the child. However, it is imperative that you do this in consultation with a dietitian/nutritionist. Your child's growing body has special requirements for fats that an adult may not. Researchers are still not sure exactly what these requirements are, and so a fat-restricted diet for a child should be undertaken cautiously.

The newly developed fat substitutes such as olestra make very little sense in the diet of normal children, and this includes picky eaters. Their safety over the long haul has yet to be proven. It takes very little effort to create a menu using naturally occurring foodstuffs without having to resort to artificial substitutes. A diet that contains a balance of animal and vegetable fats does not require any artificial additions or substitutions.

For the rest of us who do not have a cholesterol problem, we need to eat a prudent diet. Remember, eggs have recently been given a bit of a reprieve. Some scientists now feel that the restriction of three to four eggs per week may be too strict for most people, including children. We should avoid high-cholesterol foods but don't need to subject ourselves or our children to every zero cholesterol item on the shelf. Children need some of it to grow and thrive. Do I need to say it again? *Everything in moderation.*

FAT

The issues regarding dietary fat are really similar to those for cholesterol. The possibility of a link between fat intake and breast cancer is still controversial, but it has added a new concern for women. In recent years fat substitutes have been developed and more low-fat and no-fat products are appearing on our grocery shelves. In fact, I and my patients' parents can no longer find yogurt made from whole milk in our local store.

If your child is obese, you should be working closely with your pediatrician to develop an appropriate diet and exercise regimen. Often the goal is not weight loss, but merely holding the current weight and allowing the child to grow into it. This is usually something that you should not try to undertake on your own. Ask for professional help.

If you or someone else in the household is overweight, please don't put the entire family on a no-fat diet. Your picky eater still needs fat for growth and unfortunately most people have learned that fat makes food taste better. Remember, we are trying to return the fun to eating for your child and the family, and overrestricting the fat content of the diet may make it a bit less enjoyable to eat. Unless otherwise specified, the food recommendations at the end of this chapter do not imply low-fat or no-fat items.

SALT

While there is ample scientific evidence of a causal relationship between excess salt intake and high blood pressure in young animals (mostly mice), the data for humans are not so clear-cut. However, it is suspected that there probably are certain children who have inherited a tendency toward high blood pressure for whom a diet heavy in salt might hasten the onset of the problem. Unfortunately, scientists can't tell us exactly who these children are. It would seem sensible for us all to avoid foods high in salt and refrain from placing a salt shaker on the table. The acquired taste for salt can be powerful, but it is possible to wean oneself (or one's child) down to more reasonable levels of intake. Prepared soups (not claiming to be low-salt) and salty snacks, including pickles, are definitely things to avoid for your picky eater and yourself. As you might expect, going overboard in serving your child only low-salt and no-salt foods may be unsafe and the food may be tasteless. Salt is a necessary nutritional element, but the menus suggested in this chapter will provide an adequate intake.

If your family has high blood pressure, your child should already have been tested. There is no child too young to have his blood pressure taken. If it is elevated, your pediatrician may suggest further tests. The diet again is one of moderation. No salt on the table, no salty snacks or salty prepared food.

FIBER

The last five or ten years have seen an increased awareness of the role of fiber in a healthy diet. Your grandmother would have called it roughage, and apparently she already knew that eating foods that contained some indigestible (at least for humans) vegetable material helped with bowel function. She didn't suspect that it might also help to reduce the risk of bowel and other cancers.

The scientific data on fiber are still a bit shaky, but a healthy diet should include such things as whole grains, dried beans and peas, and fruits and vegetables, particularly served in their skins. But be cautious about giving your child a high-fiber diet. Small children often don't digest these kinds of foods well, in part because they aren't real good at chewing them up. The result can be abdominal discomfort and gas. If some of your child's few favorite foods would qualify as roughage, that is fine, but if he is complaining of bellyaches and seems gassy, then this may be one of the rare situations in which you should offer the child some slightly different food from the rest of the family. A few less whole grains, and a bit more peeling of fruits and vegetables for the small child who seems to be gassy. By the time he is five or six, he probably should be able to digest all the things that the adults can.

NATURAL AND HEALTH FOODS

If you shop frequently at a natural or health food store, I would caution you to be an informed consumer. Often there is nothing inherently different or better about a product bought in one of these stores when compared with the usual grocery store, except price. Brown rice is brown rice; it may be cheaper in bulk, but not always. Reading labels and asking a few questions can usually tell you if there are any advantages to the "natural" product that you are buying for your family. Unless the retailer has firsthand knowledge of the farmer's agricultural practices, you don't really know what is meant by "organic." If you are concerned about pesticides and other chemical additives getting into the food chain, then a truly "organically grown" food may be more appealing, but you may need to speak directly to the farmer. In many parts of the country, farmers' markets are appearing where you can buy directly from the grower. Foods bought in this way are often fresher, and you usually have the advantage of meeting the grower face to face.

If the tremendous waste of natural resources that characterizes the packaging of grocery store items seems appalling, then a natural food store will help you to be more environmentally conscious in your purchases because you can often buy in bulk and bring your own recyclable container. These stores may also have a broader selection of less commonly prepared foods, but don't assume that everything in a health food store is nutritionally superior.

GETTING DOWN TO BASICS

The general requirements of basic meal planning are really very simple. One does not have to be a rocket scientist to understand the principles of the four food groups. In fact, I would be very surprised if you hadn't already learned them by the time you were in third or fourth grade. Hopefully, most of your education about nutrition came at home because your mother (and/or your father) were presenting you with a healthy array of foods. Some of your knowledge may have come from a health or science teacher. The real problem is having the fortitude to adhere consistently to these principles day in and day out while the rest of your life swirls around you.

Unfortunately, in recent years the presentation of the nutritional basics has become unnecessarily complex with the introduction of the "food pyramid." While I am sure this addition to our educational concepts was well intentioned, I think that it introduces a sense of confusion that could have been avoided. I suspect that part of the rationale behind the food pyramid rests

with the desire to present a diet in terms of its daily requirements. I think it is much simpler and probably better to consider your nutritional presentation *one meal at a time.* For this
reason you are not going to see any food pyramids, pie graphs,
or tables of daily requirements in this chapter.

To my very simpleminded way of thinking, meal planning
boils down to the following principle: *Your family should be presented with three meals that each contain adequate amounts of the
four basic groups.*

Many of the pamphlets and books that I reviewed in preparing this book only suggest three food groups for breakfast, or
give you the option to include the meat or meat-alternative
group in only two of the meals. However, I think that for a
family with a picky eater, it is advantageous to present all four
food groups at all three meals. For example, breakfast and lunch
should include foods such as egg, cheese, or peanut butter from
the meat group, in addition to the more-traditional milk, bread,
and fruit. This may mean that you are fixing bigger meals, and
there may be some waste, but, remember, one of our goals is to
offer your child a broad variety. Let's at least give him some
choices from all the food groups at a time of day when he is
likely to be hungriest.

While your picky eater will probably eat better at the first
two meals of the day than at the last, you never can tell! Hence,
each meal should be as complete and varied a presentation as is
reasonable under the circumstances. If you think of your dietary
presentation as a daily event, there is some temptation to post-
pone some of the nutritional elements until later in the day. For
most picky eaters this is when they are least likely to eat. To be
safe each meal should be able to stand on its own and contain
all four food groups.

I know that adhering to this principle can be a little difficult
when it comes to breakfast because at times it is hard to include

a meat or meat alternative in the morning. But if *moderation* is a good concept to remember in meal planning, so is *flexibility*. Cold pizza for breakfast is one of my favorites. Just because they don't advertise it on television as a breakfast food doesn't mean that pizza isn't a good nutritional choice. It is! The same could be said for grilled-cheese sandwiches. Some days the whole family could have a breakfast-style meal in the evening, with waffles, ham and eggs, omelets, etc. Loosen up and occasionally climb out of the rut. Your picky eater may respond positively to novelty. While most mornings it would be wise to offer something like an egg or peanut butter, this is not an absolute necessity if your child does tend to eat something from this food group at one of his other meals. Your child really needs to be presented with something from the protein group twice each day. However, it makes more sense to satisfy his morning hunger with a complete meal (all four food groups) at breakfast than to give him two bowls of cereal.

MILK

As you look at the menus in chapter 18, you may be surprised at how little milk you should be offering your child. The one- to three-year-old needs only one-half cup of milk per meal and the three- to six-year-old needs only three-quarters of a cup. If your child drinks much more, he may have a drinking problem. Keep the volume of milk down. If your child complains of thirst after he has finished his allotted one-half or three-quarters cup, put a cup of water on the table along with his milk—and stick to your guns!

If your child appears to be lactose intolerant, you may have to treat the milk with an enzyme additive. It is sometimes difficult to diagnose lactose intolerance, but if your child seems to be gassy, complains of bloating, or has frequent loose stools when he drinks milk or eats ice cream or yogurt, he may have the problem. Often it is temporary and frequently follows a bout of gastroenteritis ("intestinal flu"). You should discuss this possible diagnosis with your pediatrician, but it has been my experience that laboratory testing is usually not necessary. If your child seems better on the lactose-reduced milk, then you have the most likely explanation. Cheese should not cause a problem, but yogurt, although lower in lactose content than milk, may contain enough to cause a problem. Ice cream is often a major contributor to symptoms.

Every several months you might want to have a trial period back on untreated milk or yogurt to see if your child is still intolerant. Usually, the condition improves with time, although it is not unusual for it to fluctuate over a period of years for reasons that are sometimes mysterious.

If your child won't drink milk, I think it is perfectly all right to flavor it with strawberry or chocolate syrup. If this is not successful, then about one-quarter to one-half cup of yogurt, or a slice or two of cheese, at breakfast and lunch will help meet your child's need for calcium and the other important nutrients found in milk. Do not offer him juice at his meals as a replacement. If he won't drink milk, water is his only alternative. The possibility of a calcium supplement should be discussed with your pediatrician. I have found that these are a nuisance and generally unnecessary after I have reviewed the child's dietary intake over a two- or three-week period.

BREAD OR BREAD ALTERNATIVE

This category is probably the easiest to include in a family menu. Baked goods and pasta are often on the short list of favorites for many picky eaters. As I mentioned in the section on fiber, do not attempt to have all the food in this category be whole grain. Many children will not be able to adequately digest a high-fiber diet and may become gassy or develop diarrhea. In addition, there is some evidence that a diet overly weighted to whole grains may actually interfere with the absorption of some minor, but essential, nutrients.

Do not attempt to fulfill the requirement for this food group by providing your picky eater with a slice of bread or two at every meal just in case he doesn't eat what everyone else is having. Remember, we want to create a situation in which your child is encouraged to do the correct thing. If the meal planned for the family includes a portion of sliced bread, then your picky eater will be included in the offering, but do not serve bread to him as a misguided backup.

Some meals can use your child's favorite pasta shape as part of a mixture or in a casserole that also includes items from the vegetable and/or meat groups. This may encourage him to become a bit more familiar with the vegetables he has shunned. Remember that when it comes to eating, familiarity *does not* breed contempt. However, don't taint his favorites at every meal. Mixing your child's beloved macaroni with eggplant every time you serve it is just plain mean. Don't do it!

Sandwiches, of course, are another way to use a popular bread item as a vehicle for carrying less-favorite items into your picky eater's field of interest. Some evening meals can even consist of sandwiches for everyone. These can often be quick meals for evenings when preparation time is at a minimum.

Flatbreads such as tortillas and pita pockets offer another way to include the bread group in a meal that can be interesting for both adults and children. While sometimes messy, these ethnic breads can provide the hands-on appeal that even some picky eaters will enjoy. Other nontraditional presentations of the bread group include cold leftover pizza for breakfast (one of my favorites, as I've said before) and pancakes or waffles for supper.

To repeat a previous warning, *breakfast cereals are to be served only at breakfast*. These are foods that are particularly popular with picky eaters and many families continue to offer them as snacks and at other meals. *Don't!* Unless you have planned to serve everyone at the table breakfast cereal as part of your meal plan for supper (which I hope you won't), then stick to your guns. Breakfast cereal only at breakfast.

Presweetened cereals aren't my favorite when it comes to good nutrition, but I would not put them on my forbidden list either. Steer your child to the most nutritionally complete breakfast cereals (read the side panels), and try to use fruit (fresh or dried) on them for flavor enhancement, but don't be pigheaded. One bowl of presweetened cereal with milk as part of a breakfast is not a nutritional disaster. Three or four bowls per day are!

FRUITS AND VEGETABLES

Traditionally, this food group, at least the vegetable side of it, has been the most difficult for parents of picky eaters. However, if you realize that fruits are often very good sources of some of the vitamins and other nutritional elements that we usually associate with vegetables, this may make things a bit easier.

Because cooking sometimes diminishes the food value of fruits and vegetables, they are often best served raw. In fact, many children prefer them served this way. But uncooked vegetables can pose a choking hazard for small children, and safety should be considered in your presentation. While I have encouraged you to prepare only one meal for the family, I don't think that it is unreasonable to serve the picky eater uncooked carrots and cook them for the family, or vice versa. This should not present an excessive amount of extra preparation time and may make the mealtime more pleasant.

Salads are often a good way to fill the requirement for this food group. They can be served as a first course to take advantage of the child's hunger while the rest of the meal is being prepared. The bowl can then remain on the table until the meal is over.

While I don't want to get caught claiming that ketchup is a vegetable, a thick or chunky tomato sauce is one method of including some vegetable components in the meal. Meals that center on a mixture of elements that include vegetables can be a very popular way of presenting them. Here I am talking about dishes like vegetarian lasagnas and chilies. Even pizzas can provide an appealing platform for presenting vegetables to the picky eater and your family.

As discussed in chapter 15, fruit can be served at the end of the meal to round out its nutritional completeness. Some authors and nutritionists suggest serving the fruit along with the other components of the meal. I think it is better to hold off until most of the family have finished the bulk of their meal before presenting the fruit. This delay slightly increases the chance that the picky eater may get adventuresome and try something on his no list. But, remember, there should be no hint that you are holding out fruit as a reward. You are serving the fruit last, just because that's the way you do it. There should be no hint of contingency.

MEAT AND MEAT ALTERNATES

This is the other food group that picky eaters traditionally avoid. Sometimes this is because small children often lack the chewing skills and patience to eat even the most tender cut of beef. Make sure that your child can handle safely the meat that you are offering. I have known some parents who have asked their butcher to cut or shave the meat into paper-thin slices to make things easier for the child.

Baked chicken nuggets or fish sticks are often more appealing to children and may be tolerable for most adults. Family meals are a compromise and presenting meat in a more child-friendly manner for some meals shouldn't be too difficult. Children usually enjoy something that they can eat off a stick, and a chicken or turkey leg is a natural equivalent. Skewered meats (and vegetables) offer another opportunity to eat off a stick, but make sure that your child is mature enough to be trusted with such a sharp stick. Hot dogs (made of beef, pork, turkey, chicken, or soy protein) have received some bad publicity for all of the horrible things that they sometimes contain. While they may not be on the A list for culinary excellence, they are certainly not without nutritional value and can be included occasionally as an offering. The potential for choking, however, can be high for small children, and hot dogs should be cut up carefully to minimize this risk.

Don't forget that eggs are also in this group, and you may find that omelets and quiches have a broad appeal in your family. They present a texture that many children find easy to eat. Now that we believe that their contribution to the cholesterol problem is somewhat less than we did a few years ago, eggs can be a big help in rounding out your balanced meals. I think a limit of one egg per day is reasonable until we learn more about their impact on health.

Cooked dry beans and peas also fall into this meat category and have become increasingly popular as more families and individuals are becoming less inclined to eat meat. Chilies and cold bean salads can offer appealing ways to present this nutritional component and allow for easy combination with members of the vegetable group. Of course, your picky eater is likely to eat just his favorite bits and leave the rest behind, but some day he may try some of the "strangers" in the mixture by accident or because he figures that they may not be so bad after all because they seem to keep showing up with his old "friends."

Peanut butter and cheese are also members in good standing of this food group but they deserve some special cautions. First, peanut butter does stick to the roof of your mouth (and your child's) and so can pose a choking risk for the child under the age of three. Remember that you shouldn't be feeding these little people unattended. Second, cheese is a major contribution to constipation, and if this is a problem for your child, you may want to keep cheese as a minor player in your menu planning. Finally, like sliced bread, many parents offer their picky eater sliced cheese as a backup at meals when the child has not eaten the meat that was served. If you continue to offer the path of least resistance by giving him the alternative of a favored food, you have removed hunger as his motivation to try something on his no list. For your child to make healthy choices, he must be given a healthy variety, not monotony.

THE VEGETARIAN FAMILY

By eliminating meat from your diet, you obviously limit the choices of food that you can offer your child. This usually is not much of a problem because picky eaters often include meat on their no list. However, you might want to discuss your diet with a dietitian to make sure that your menu plans are nutritionally complete. This precaution is particularly important if you have only recently become vegetarians. If your family has kept to a vegetarian diet for a generation or two, then it is probably safe to assume that your selection of meat alternates can provide enough nutritional elements to support the growth and development of normal children.

For the child between ages two and five years, meat offers a source of iron that is easy to absorb. It is difficult to create a vegetarian diet that will provide your child with enough of this important nutritional element. Iron is found in many tissues throughout the body, but its supply is critical in the formation of red blood cells. Insufficient dietary iron will initially cause anemia, and if not corrected more serious health problems.

While meat can also be an important source of protein, most small children get enough protein from the milk group. However, a rapidly growing teenager may have difficulty meeting his body's protein requirement by eating a vegetarian diet. I cannot emphasize enough how important it is to avoid overrestriction in the meat and meat alternate group. If you also eliminate dairy products and eggs from your offerings, your child's diet is very likely to be incomplete in both iron and protein.

Even more restrictive menus such as a macrobiotic diet must be condemned as being unhealthy for growing children. Do not be fooled by the apparent health of the advocates of these bizarre diets. They may not be as healthy as you think, and, more important, they are adults who have finished growing. Your child's nutritional requirements are broader and more complex. An overly restrictive diet could eliminate a nutritional element that may not be terribly important to the health of an adult, but may be critical for your child's continued growth and mental development. Sometimes it can be difficult to evaluate the credentials of someone who claims to be a nutritionist because he or she may have accumulated a very impressive collection of degrees. Before making changes in your child's diet that are based on what you suspect is nontraditional advice, seek several other opinions from registered dietitians and your pediatrician.

SUGGESTED MENUS

On the next few pages, you will find some suggested menus for breakfast, lunch, and dinner. The amounts next to each item should be viewed as ballpark figures. They are intended as first servings of the foods that a child is likely to eat. With a few exceptions your child may have a second helping of his favorites *if* he has finished the token servings of his unfavorites. You will note that each meal has a representative from the four food groups.

The breakfasts may seem like large meals, but the items from the "meat" category are optional and are intended to be offered to the child who eats his best meal in the morning. I also have not suggested token amounts for breakfast because there should be no "seconds" on most of the items, particularly eggs and dry cereal. The amount of milk listed is a combination of beverage and that poured on cereal.

You will see that there are two amounts listed for each menu item. The one in the lefthand column is intended for a child aged one to three years, and the amount in the righthand column for a child of three to five. These are intended as rough guidelines, and if your two-and-a-half-year-old is as big as most four-year-olds, you probably should be serving the larger portion.

When I suggest a "cup" of fruit, I mean a piece of fresh fruit that would fit in a cup container. A small apple or peach would be a good example of what I am talking about. If you don't feel comfortable eyeballing these amounts, particularly for odd-shaped foods such as bananas, you may want to use a measuring cup—once. Remember, I have discouraged you from weighing and measuring your child's food on a regular basis. Certainly don't let your child see you doing it.

Notice that at the bottom of each menu are suggested "token" serving sizes for certain foods that are likely to be on your child's no list. These are portions of unfavorites that I feel are small enough to give your child some hope of finishing them and thereby qualifying him for seconds on his favorites.

SAMPLE BREAKFASTS

AGE 1–3 YEARS	AGE 3–5 YEARS
1. 1/2 cup milk	3/4 cup milk
1/4 cup fruit	1/2 cup fruit
1/4 cup dry cereal	1/3 cup dry cereal
1 egg	1 egg
2. 1/2 cup yogurt	3/4 cup yogurt
4 oz citrus juice	4 oz citrus juice
1/2 slice of toast	3/4 slice of toast
2 tbsp peanut butter	3 tbsp peanut butter
3. 1/2 cup milk	3/4 cup milk
1/4 cup fruit	1/2 cup fruit
1/2 waffle (4-inch)	3/4 waffle (4-inch)
1 (1-oz) slice of cheese	1-1/2 oz slice of cheese

171

SAMPLE LUNCHES

AGE 1–3 YEARS	AGE 3–5 YEARS

1. 1/2 cup milk
1/4 cup fruit*
1/2 slice bread
1 slice meat or cheese
   or 2 tbsp peanut butter
	3/4 cup milk
	1/2 cup fruit
	3/4 slice bread
	1 1/2 slice meat or cheese
	   or 3 tbsp peanut butter

2. 1/2 cup yogurt 1/4 cup fresh vegetable* 1/4 cup macaroni and cheese	3/4 cup yogurt 1/2 cup fresh vegetable 1/2 cup macaroni and cheese
3. 1/2 cup milk 1/4 cup fruit* 1/8 small pizza	3/4 cup milk 1/2 cup fruit 1/4 small pizza
4. 1/2 cup milk 1/4 cup fruit* 6 corn chips or crackers 1 cut-up hot dog	3/4 cup milk 1/2 cup fruit* 6 corn chips or crackers 1 hot dog/bun

5. 1/2 cup yogurt
1/4 cup fruit*
1/2 cup chili or
   vegetable-bean soup
	3/4 cup yogurt
	1/2 cup fruit
	3/4 to 1 cup chili or
	   vegetable-bean soup

*Token amounts of these items would be about 1 tablespoon for 1- to 3-year-olds and 2 tablespoons for 3- to 5-year-olds.

SAMPLE SUPPERS

AGE 1–3 YEARS	AGE 3–5 YEARS
1. 1/2 cup milk 1/2 cup mixed green salad* (with dressing) 1/4 cup spaghetti with meatballs or sauce	3/4 cup milk 1/2 cup mixed green salad* (with dressing) 1/2 cup spaghetti with meatballs or sauce
2. 1/2 cup milk 1/4 cup vegetables* 1/2 hamburger with bun	3/4 cup milk 1/2 cup vegetables* 3/4 to 1 hamburger with bun
3. 1/2 cup milk 1/4 cup fruit* 1/2 burrito or taco	3/4 cup milk 1/2 cup fruit* 3/4 burrito or taco
4. 1/2 cup milk 1/2 cup vegetarian lasagna 1 scoop ice cream with fruit	3/4 cup milk 3/4 cup vegetarian lasagna 1 scoop ice cream with fruit
5. 1/2 cup milk 1/4 cup vegetable* 1/2 cup baked French fries 1 chicken leg	3/4 cup milk 1/2 cup vegetable* 3/4 cup baked French fries 1 chicken leg

*Token amounts of these items would be about 1 tablespoon for 1- to 3-year-olds and 2 tablespoons for 3- to 5-year-olds.

SNACKS

I suggest that of the two daily snacks, one be from the fruit-vegetable group and the other from the bread group. The beverage served with the snack could be fruit juice or milk, but try to keep your child to no more than four cups of milk per day (including meals) and no more than two cups of juice (not including citrus juice at breakfast).

MID-MORNING

AGE 1–3 YEARS	AGE 3–5 YEARS
1. 4 oz juice 1/4 cup raisins	4 oz juice 1/2 cup raisins
2. 4 oz milk 3 crackers	4 oz milk 4 crackers
3. 4 oz juice 1/4 cup orange slices	4 oz milk 1/2 cup orange slices

MID-AFTERNOON

AGE 1–3 YEARS	AGE 3–5 YEARS
1. 4 oz juice 2 cookies	4 oz juice 3 cookies
2. 4 oz milk 1/4 cup cucumber spears	4 oz juice 1/2 cup cucumber spears
3. 4 oz milk 3/4 pretzel (salt removed)	4 oz juice 1 pretzel (large)

VITAMINS AND
OTHER BAD IDEAS

Almost every family that I work with who has a poor eater is either giving the child vitamins or asks me about them. My advice is almost always to avoid giving extra vitamins. My reasons are several. First, your child's diet, strange and erratic as it may seem, will provide him adequate vitamins *and* there is no evidence that additional vitamins will do any good, nor will they prevent disease. While billions of dollars are spent on vitamins each year in this country, and millions of people take vitamins every day, their effectiveness in normal children offered a normal diet has not been consistently proven. If the child is anemic or has a specific medical problem, then vitamins may play a very important role, but remember this book is written for normal, healthy children who by definition don't need added vitamins.

I know that there are physicians who recommend vitamins for children who are poor eaters because they feel that the added vitamins couldn't hurt and may give the parents enough confidence to follow through on a program similar to the one that I have outlined. However . . .

VITAMINS CAN HURT

Vitamins are not totally innocuous. Given in their usual dosages they have few, if any, side effects. However, taken in overdose they can result in serious complications, even to the point of death, particularly if the vitamin preparations also contain iron. Because the vitamins designed for children are often candylike in their appearance and taste, they are one of the most common medications involved in pediatric overdoses.

The victim of the overdose may not be the child for whom the medication was intended. It could be a younger (or older) sibling or a playmate or neighbor. While the dosage required for fatality may be quite large, when iron is involved, this can be achieved with medication amounts found around the house.

Another common problem results from the similarity between vitamins and other medications. The child likes the taste of the vitamins and the praise that he gets for taking them. When he finds his grandmother's heart medicine in her pocketbook, he naturally assumes that they will taste good and have a positive effect on his life. Nothing could be farther from the truth.

If you decide to ignore my suggestion about vitamins, at least avoid getting the ones with iron unless they have been specifically recommended or prescribed by your child's pediatrician. Then keep them with their safety caps in place in an inaccessible (for the child) location. Remember, children know how to move chairs and use them as ladders. Take every opportunity to remind the child that he only takes *his* medicine and that he is not to take anyone else's medication and should certainly consult with you before taking anything from anyone other than yourselves.

THE WRONG MESSAGES

By offering your child pills when he doesn't eat well, your actions are sending him some messages that you may wish to reconsider. In administering vitamins you are saying, "If things aren't going well, just reach for a bottle of pills. They will make things better." Is this really the solution that you want your child to consider when things in his life aren't working well? Do you really want him thinking about drugs as one of his first solutions when his life isn't going the way he would like? It may seem like a giant leap from multicolored chewable vitamins in funny shapes to drug abuse, but I would urge you to take a hard look at your own attitude toward medications.

As a busy practicing pediatrician, I will tell you that some days I spend more time trying to talk families out of using medications than I do in prescribing them. In medical school I was taught what medications could and couldn't do and that they should be used only when absolutely necessary. I was told to always consider the risks or side effects of whatever treatment I was going to suggest. Believe me, it is not a giant leap to go from chewable vitamins to popping pills as an adolescent. I won't guarantee that by not giving vitamins to your toddler, you will avoid a teenage drug problem. There are too many other factors. However, if you have shown your child that you think drugs are the answer to a problem (especially when they really aren't), you certainly aren't setting a good example. There is no getting around it—vitamins are drugs. Your choice to give them to your child should be made carefully, and vitamins should be treated with the same respect as any other drug in your medicine cabinet.

MY BASIC MESSAGE

If you give your child vitamins when he doesn't eat well, then you have not really read and accepted the basic message of this book. You are still harboring the notion that it is your job to ensure that your child ingests a balanced diet every day. You lack the trust in your child's innate ability to take in a balanced diet over the long haul. It is very likely that this insecurity will spill over into your behavior at family meals, and it will be difficult for you to avoid the pitfall of giving the child whatever he wants so that you can watch him eat. You will find it hard to keep quiet during family meals and will run the risk of talking about your child's eating habits and ruining a nice family gathering. Before you consider giving vitamins, please go back to the beginning of the book and read chapters 4, 5, and 6 again.

IF YOU MUST . . .

By giving your child vitamins, you are continuing to say to your child that there is something wrong with him and his eating habits. This is not true. Remember, these strange eating patterns are normal for young children. It is not your job to continually point out your child's failings. Your role is to point out his strengths and to emphasize the attributes that make him special. It doesn't make any sense when it comes to eating habits to take your child aside and say, "Here, there is something wrong with you. Take this pill."

I realize that despite my best efforts, there are some parents who are going to cave in and give their child vitamins. Of all the crimes we parents can commit, giving your child vitamins is one of the more minor ones. If giving your child vitamins is going to give you that extra shot of confidence that I have been unable to provide, then fine—go ahead. If a pill a day will allow you to present a balanced diet and keep quiet about your child's eating habits, then I think we are in the "lesser of two evils" category. I guess I would have to admit that the end justifies the means.

Remember to downplay their importance when you are talking with your child about vitamins. Please don't tell your child, "I guess it's okay if you don't eat your green beans, you had your vitamin today." Just clam up and don't say anything. Keep them in a safe place, with their safety caps closed. Avoid iron-containing vitamins unless they are specifically recommended by your pediatrician. Keep the dose at "one-a-day." More is not necessarily better. You are just looking for a supplement, you are not treating a disease. And as soon as you have regained your confidence, stop them.

When you give vitamins to the child make sure you tell him the truth. Something like "Mommy is worried that when you aren't eating all your food that you aren't getting enough vitamins. Dr. Wilkoff tells me not to worry, that your eating is fine, but I still worry, and I would like you to take the vitamins, so that I won't worry so much." I hope that is a fair and honest statement that you can live with. Certainly, if your child balks and doesn't want to take them, do not push. In this situation vitamins are not a medication that should be forced.

OTHER NUTRITIONAL SUPPLEMENTS

Sometimes parents aren't satisfied with giving their child vitamins when he isn't eating. They then turn to some of the nutritional supplements that can be bought without prescription. These range all the way from things like a milkshake that claims to replace your breakfast to special formulas that are used to supplement the nutrition of children with certain chronic diseases. While there are some legitimate uses for these special formulas, they are not intended for the normal child and should be condemned on the same grounds as vitamins. They really don't address the basic issues and can be dangerous if relied upon for complete nutrition, particularly the breakfast drinks. Remember that if you present your child with a broad variety of foods in appropriate amounts, then he can be trusted to eat a balanced diet. It may take several weeks for him to complete the balancing act, but he can and will do it. Don't forget that if you present your child a variety of foods, he will learn to eat a variety of foods. However, if all he gets is an enriched milkshake, there is no incentive for him to try other foods.

"Meal replacement bars" are also a bad idea, because while they may provide your child adequate quantities of most nutritional elements, they do nothing to promote his development of good eating habits. If you are trying to create a banquet atmosphere for at least one meal each day, the image of your child sitting at his place munching on a high-energy bar doesn't seem to fit.

Protein supplements can be extremely dangerous because they may provide a protein load that your child's body is incapable of handling. Yes, there is such a thing as too much protein. Small children don't need as much dietary protein as adolescents, and their kidneys aren't equipped to process the excess protein.

These liquid supplements have additional problems in that if the child drinks them, they will feel full and not want to eat when mealtime comes around. This leaves the child caught in a vicious cycle, because the solution you have chosen for your child's poor eating will continue to contribute to his poor appetite by filling him up. At some time you are going to have to stop these supplements and let him get hungry for real food. When are you going to do it? My answer is "Before you start!"

In addition to being potentially dangerous and illogical, the use of liquid supplements delays the implementation of basic suggestions outlined in this book. Provide a variety of real food in adequate amounts. Serve it in a relaxed atmosphere and put appropriate limits on drinking and snacking. While I can waver a little on vitamins, I see no justification for the use of liquid supplements for the normal child.

Very often the natural approach is the best. Vitamins and protein and mineral supplements really aren't natural in this sense, even though they come from the health food store. If presented a proper diet in a relaxed and pleasant atmosphere, your child will over the long haul take in the proper nutrients, and vitamins and supplements are not necessary.

PHONY FOODS

Diet drinks, diet foods, sugar and fat substitutes, have no place in your family's diet. If your attitude is that your child can indulge in diet soft drinks because they contain so few calories that they won't interfere with your child's appetite, you are wrong. The volume of the drink itself will blunt his appetite. If you think that it is okay to allow your child to eat potato chips in the late afternoon because you have bought a brand that claims to be lower in fat and salt, you need to realize that this is only relative to other potato chips. They are still a food that is inherently a poor choice for a snack. Fruit would be a better alternative.

Foods that claim to be improved by the addition of a fat substitute also make little sense for the healthy family. There are so many alternative "natural" foods that it should be easy to avoid the foods that are high in fat without having to resort to the trickery that is inherent in fat substitutes. Your honesty and integrity in your food selection for your family will set a valuable example for your picky eater.

SOME FINAL THOUGHTS

As I sit down to put the finishing touches on this, my first book, the state of Maine is struggling to free herself from the frigid grip of the worst ice storm of the century. Those of us lucky enough to have had our electrical power restored after four days are beginning to return to our routines. Thousands of my fellow Mainers are still searching for generators, stoking their woodstoves, and hauling water. I haven't had a call from the worried parent of a picky eater for more than a week and a half.

This meteorological catastrophe has changed the lifestyles of families with the crack of an ice-encrusted limb. Suddenly, everyone in the house is content to be eating whatever is available, and more pleased if it happens to be warm. Every meal is eaten by candlelight, and families linger at the table for an hour or more, talking, playing games, enjoying the chance to be together. There is no rush to get up and turn on the television—it doesn't work. Meals have become social occasions eagerly anticipated as entertainment and as distractions from the monotony of cabin fever. Concerns about frozen pipes and thawing freezers take priority. No one seems to be worried whether Zachary has eaten his peas or not.

Picky eating is a phenomenon unique to cultures of plenty. When stripped of its excesses by political or natural disaster, a society can no longer offer its members the luxury of choice. Of course, I don't want your community to suffer through an ice storm or hurricane just so that your family will be forced to change its attitudes toward mealtime behavior. I suspect that the same old habits would return when the electricity came back on. However, I hope that having read this book, you will find it easier to put your child's picky eating into proper perspective and make the appropriate changes in your behavior. Remember, refusing to eat his broccoli isn't going to kill him. Your responsibility stops with presenting him a variety of nutritious foods in a pleasant atmosphere and setting healthy limits on drinking and snacking.

Don't wait for an ice storm to cut off your electricity. Put a candle on the table tonight. Then serve the meal, sit back, and enjoy your family. Mealtimes with a picky eater can be fun.

INDEX